The Ponytail Girls

The Impossible Christmas Present

LEGACY PRESS

The Ponytail Girls

The Impossible Christmas Present

Bonnie Compton Hanson

Dedication

To each girl who reads this book
and becomes a PT, filling with joy your own life
and the lives of all you meet.

THE PONYTAIL GIRLS/
BOOK 2: THE IMPOSSIBLE CHRISTMAS PRESENT
©2002 by Legacy Press, second printing
ISBN 1-58411-030-9
Legacy reorder# LP48042

Legacy Press
P.O. Box 261129
San Diego, CA 92196

Illustrator: Aline Heiser

Scriptures are from the *Holy Bible: New International Version*
(North American Edition), ©1973, 1978, 1984 by the
International Bible Society. Used by permission of
Zondervan Bible Publishers.

Printed in the United States of America

Contents

~ Introduction ~

Welcome to the Ponytail Girls! Whether you wear a ponytail or not you can share in the adventures of Sam Pearson and her friends, the PTs (that's short for Ponytail Girls!). Just like you, the PTs love sports and shopping and fun with their friends at school.

The PTs also want to live in a way that is pleasing to God. So when they have problems and conflicts, they look to God and His Word, the Bible. They might also seek help from their parents, their pastor or their Sunday school class teacher, just like you do.

Each chapter in this book presents a new problem for your PTs to solve. Then there is a Bible story to help explain the Christian value that the PTs learned. A Bible memory verse is included for you to practice and share.

There may be words in this book that are new to you, especially some Bible names and Spanish words. Look them up in the Glossary on page 199, then use the syllables in the brackets to sound out the words.

In addition to the stories, in each chapter you will find questions to answer and fun quizzes, puzzles and other activities. Also, at the end of each chapter starting with Chapter 1, you get clues to add to the Advent Calendar. See if you can guess what it says before all the clues are in!

The fun doesn't end with the stories. At the end of the book, there are more Ponytail Girls activities. If you didn't start your own Ponytail Girls club after you read the first book, there is information on how to do so now, along with membership cards.

This second Ponytail Girls book begins just after Thanksgiving. The next three books continue on through the school year and into the following summer. So as soon as you finish this book, Sam and her friends want to share more Ponytail Girls adventures with you. Now turn to page 11 to meet the PTs!

And Merry Christmas!

Meet the Ponytail Girls!

· WHO ARE THEY? ·

The PTs are girls your age who enjoy school, church, shopping and being with their friends and family. They also love meeting new friends. Friends just like you! You will like being a part of their lives.

The Ponytail Girls all attend Madison Middle School in the small town of Circleville. They're all also members of Miss Kotter's Sunday school class at nearby Faith Church on Sunday mornings. On Sunday evenings, they attend the special Zone 56 group for guys and girls in fifth and sixth grade. Their pastor is Rev. J. T. McConahan, and their youth leader is Pastor Andrew Garretti, whom they call "Pastor Andy."

Sam and Sara grew up in Circleville. Le's and LaToya's families moved into their neighborhood last year. When Sam and Sara met them at school, they invited them to church. Now it would be difficult for them to imagine not being Ponytail Girls! And as each new member joins, she feels the same way.

How did the PTs get their club name? Well, as you can see from their pictures, they all wear a ponytail of one kind or another. So that's what their other friends and families started calling them just for fun. Then one day LaToya shortened it to "PTs." Now that's what they all call themselves!

The PTs' club meetings are held whenever they can all get together. The girls have a secret motto: PT4JC, which means "Ponytails for Jesus Christ." But most of the time they don't want to keep secrets. They want to share with everyone the Good News about their best friend, Jesus.

So have fun sharing in your PTs' adventures. Laugh with them in their silly times, think and pray with them through their problems. And learn with them that the answers to all problems can be found right in God's Word. Keep your Bible and a sharpened pencil handy. Sam and the others are waiting for you!

GET TO KNOW THE PTS

Sam Pearson *has a long blond ponytail, sparkling blue eyes and a dream: she wants to play professional basketball. She also likes to design clothes. Sam's name is Samantha, but her friends and family just call her "Sam" for short. Sam's little brother, Petie, is 6. Joe, her dad, is great at fixing things, like cars and bikes. Her mom, Jean, bakes scrumptious cakes and pies and works at the Paws and Pooches Animal Shelter. Sneezit is the family dog.*

LaToya Thomas' *black curls are ponytailed high above her ears. That way she doesn't miss a thing going on! LaToya's into gymnastics and playing the guitar. Her big sister, Tina, is in college, training to be a nurse. Her mom is a school teacher; her dad works nights at a supermarket. Also living with the Thomases is LaToya's beloved, wheelchair-bound grandmother, Granny B.*

Le Tran *parts her glossy black hair to one side, holding it back with one small ponytail. She loves sewing, soccer and playing the violin. Her mother, Viola, a concert pianist, often plays duets with her. Her father, Daniel, died in an accident. Mrs. Tran is a Buddhist from Vietnam, but Mr. Tran became a Christian before he died. Le's mother is a new Christian.*

• Le Tran •

Sara Fields *lives down the street from Sam. She keeps her fiery, red hair from flying away by tying it into a ponytail flat against each side of her head. Sara has freckles, glasses and a great sense of humor. She loves to sing. She also loves softball, ice skating and cheerleading. Sara has a big brother, Tony, and a big dog, Tank. Both her parents are artists.*

• Sara Fields •

When **Maria Moreno** *moved in next door to Sam in September, she became the fifth PT. Maria pulls part of her long, brown hair into one topknot ponytail at the back; the rest hangs loose. She is tall, the way basketball-lover Sam would like to be! But Maria's into science, not basketball. At home, she helps her mother take*  *care of her 6-year-old twin brothers, Juan and Ricardo, and a little sister, Lolita. The Morenos all speak Spanish as well as English.*

Miss Kitty Kotter*, the girls' Sunday school teacher, is not a PT, but she is an important part of their lives both in and out of church. Miss Kotter works as a computer engineer. She also loves to go on hikes. Her boyfriend, Bob Ingram, is in the Navy, so he is out to sea most of the time. Miss Kotter calls the Bible her "how-to book" because, she says, it tells "how to" live. Miss Kitty volunteers at the Circleville Rescue Mission.*

The PTs also make new friends all the time. In this book, they will meet tall Jenna Jenkins, who wears her brown ponytail high on her head like a crown, and Sonya Silverhorse, who has a long-black braided ponytail and a sweet smile. She is in a wheelchair.

Jenna

Sonya

Get ready for fun with the PTs!

Chapter 1

I Want It All!

"Oh, I just love Christmas!" Sam Pearson said as she and her fellow PT Sara rushed out of class. "Thanksgiving's over and so is Miss Kotter's birthday. Nothing to think of now but Christmas! It's my favorite time of the year!"

She grabbed her backpack from her Madison Middle School locker as Sara pulled on her parka.

"Mine, too!" Sara agreed. "Oh, by the way, I

need to stop by the store for some notebook paper on the way home. Wanna come with me?"

Swirls of snowflakes filled the air. Piles of snow edged the sidewalk. The air smelled fresh and clean, just like...

"Christmas trees!" both girls yelled at the same time. They had spotted the vacant lot next to the store, which was filled with wonderfully-smelling evergreens — some on stands, some still tied up. "I can't wait to get a tree and decorate it!" Sam said.

The store windows were even more Christmasy. Cards and gifts and ornaments and decorations of every sort imaginable were displayed. Everything was sparkling and bright and new.

"I wish I didn't have to buy plain old notebook paper today," Sara sighed. "I want to start buying Christmas presents. Lots and lots of them!"

Sam nodded. "Me, too. I have so many things I want this year!"

When Sam reached home, her little brother, Petie, was sprawled out on the living room floor, surrounded by Christmas catalogs. "Look at the cool toys and video games in these!" he said excitedly.

Sam hung up her coat and grabbed one of the catalogs for herself. "Wow, I love these sweaters! And what a great dress for a Christmas party!"

Just then Mrs. Pearson brought in a large envelope. "This came in the mail, too," she said. "It's from Grandma Pearson."

Sam opened the envelope. "An Advent calendar! Wow!"

Her little brother wrinkled his nose. "What's that?"

"A special calendar for Christmas. See, it says, 'Happy Birthday Jesus!'

Oh, something else is in the envelope, too." Sam reached inside. "Money, Petie! Grandma sent us each $5! Awesome! I'm spending mine on Christmas stuff!"

Mrs. Pearson popped her head back into the living room and asked Sam and Petie to run down to the grocery store for some milk. "Sure!" Sam jumped up to get her coat. "C'mon, Petie. We can stop by that store where Sara and I were earlier to get some ideas for Christmas gifts. I want to buy something special for our Sunday school room this year. That would be like a birthday present for Jesus, wouldn't it?"

Sam's mom smiled and nodded her head.

By now the air was so frosty that their breath came out in white puffs. Some of the houses on their street were already ablaze with strings of bright Christmas lights.

Almost to the store, Petie suddenly stopped and pointed at a trash bin. "Hey, Sam!" he whispered. "What's that over there?"

Startled, she looked. Crouched against the building was a shivering old woman with only a plastic trash bag between her and piles of dirty snow.

Sam looked longingly at the brightly-lit stores, crammed full of new things to buy. Then she looked back at the miserable lady. Part of her said, *That old lady's none of your business, Sam. Maybe she's drunk.* But another part said, *Yes, but she's freezing. Maybe hungry and sick, too.*

"We've got to help her, Sam!" her little brother urged.

Sam sighed. "Well, we can't do much by ourselves. But Mom and Dad will know what to do." Passing right by the wonderful store with all of the Christmas gifts, they rushed in and out of the grocery store and headed home with the milk.

When their parents heard about the homeless woman they immediately called Pastor McConahan. He, in turn, contacted a doctor friend. He also called Miss Kotter, Sam's Sunday school teacher, who was the church's volunteer representative to the Circleville Rescue Mission. They all rushed down to help the homeless woman.

Later back home, Petie was all smiles. "I'm sorry that lady was sick," he said. "But I'm glad we could help her."

"Yes," Mrs. Pearson said. "After a few days in the hospital, she should be much better. She was starving to death and freezing, too. And to top it off, the poor lady had the flu. You children might have saved her life."

Sam looked at the pile of Christmas catalogs still on the floor. As she started picking them up, she thought of last Sunday's Bible story about Mary's gift to Jesus. "I guess I don't want everything for Christmas after all," she said. "I just want what Jesus wants me to have. I just want to show Him I love Him."

Her mom gave her a hug. "I think you just did, Sam," she said.

· Good News ·
from God's Word

Sam showed love by helping a sick old woman. Mary, in the following Bible story, showed her love a totally different way: by giving the most precious thing she had.

Mary's Gift of Love

FROM MATTHEW 26:6-10; JOHN 12:1-7

Mary and Martha loved Jesus so much! He was not only their wonderful friend and teacher, but He had done something for them no one else in the world could do. When their brother Lazarus died, Jesus brought him back to life again. Right out of the grave!

"Let's have a big party for Jesus!" Martha said. "We'll invite all our friends to show how thankful we are for Him."

Martha and Mary cooked and cleaned and

cooked some more. Then all their guests sat down, with Jesus in the place of honor. While Martha started serving the food, Mary went into her room. She brought back the most precious thing she owned in the world: a special perfume worth thousands of dollars. Kneeling by Jesus, she took off His dusty sandals, and poured that rich perfume over His bare feet. Then she wiped His feet dry with her own long hair. That's how much she loved Jesus!

Judas was angry. "Why did You let Mary do that, Jesus?" he fussed. "What a waste of money!"

But Jesus was glad. "Mary did this to show how much she loves Me," He said.

 ## A Verse to Remember

For to me, to live is Christ.

— ***Philippians 1:21***

What About You?

What do you want more than anything in the world?

_____

Why do you want it?

_____

If it's something that costs money, can your parents afford it, and still pay all their bills and all the other family needs?

_____

Have you prayed about it? _____

How will you feel if God answers your prayer with "no" or "wait" instead of "yes"?

_____

Jesus prayed for God's will to be done, not His own. Are you ready to pray for the same thing? _____

If God doesn't give you what you want, He will still love you just as much. Will you still love Him just as much, realizing He always knows what's best for you? _____

Christmas Is Coming

On page 25 is an Advent calendar for the last 18 days leading up to Christmas this year. Complete this Advent calendar as you read each of this book's 18 chapters.

"Advent" means "coming," as in "Christmas is coming!" The calendar has 18 spaces for pictures and 17 spaces for Secret Letters. The picture for this chapter — a Christmas wreath — is already in place.

A special secret message for Chapter 1 is on line 18: JOY! J is for Jesus, O is for Others and Y is for You. If you put your life in this order, you will be really happy!

Chapters 2 through 18 will each have a Secret Letter, but they will not be in order. When all of the Secret Letters are written on the calendar, you will be able to read them in the right order to discover the best Christmas present of all!

If you wish, you can copy the Advent calendar onto another sheet of paper, and back it with a larger sheet of colored paper or cardboard. Decorate it with Christmas stickers or in whatever way you like best!

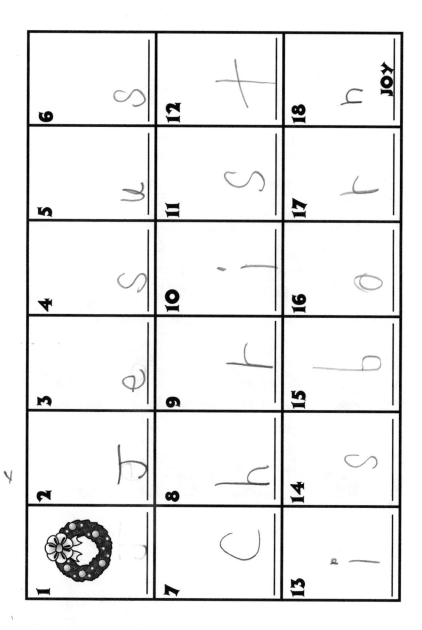

JOY

Chapter 2

Why I Love Christmas

J ust before English class ended that Friday, Sara's teacher announced, "Here is your assignment for Monday. I want each of you to do an oral report about any favorite wintertime holiday except for Christmas. We'll leave out Christmas because that would probably be everyone's choice. What are some other holiday possibilities?"

Soon the chalkboard was full of suggestions: Kwanzaa (an African-American holiday), Thanksgiving, New Year's, Hanukkah, President's Day, Tet (a Vietnamese holiday), Groundhog Day, Martin Luther King Day and many more. One boy even suggested Super Bowl Sunday, while one girl voted for her own January birthday!

Miss Anderson laughed. "Well, we'll leave those last two out, OK? You have plenty of possibilities now. So if anyone chooses Christmas instead of one of the other holidays, I'll take off points for lazy thinking, unless you convince me you have a really good reason to do so."

That Saturday, Sara helped her parents pick out a Christmas tree — the most beautiful one in the lot. Then they went to a gallery opening for new paintings by her parents, who were artists, about the life of Christ. Afterward, her big brother Tony and his pals hauled the outdoor Christmas decorations onto their roof, including a lighted sign that said, "Christmas Is Jesus' Birthday."

"Come on up and help us, Sara," Tony called. "This is fun."

Sara was afraid of heights. But then she thought, *I do want to help. I'll pray about it. Maybe it'll be OK as long as I don't look down.*

So she prayed for courage. Soon she was up on the roof stringing lights, too.

That night Sara asked, "Mom, should I really tell my English class that a winter holiday other than Christmas is my favorite? I don't want to lie, but I don't want a bad grade, either."

Mrs. Fields gave her a hug. "Keep praying about it, honey," she said. "Jesus will give you the courage to do the right thing." There was that "courage" business again!

The next day at Sunday school, Miss Kotter had great news. "Remember the homeless woman we took to the hospital?" she asked. "Her name is June Ryan, and she's much better now. She can even have visitors. I'm going to see her this afternoon, so any of you who'd like to come with me are invited. Mrs. Greenleaf is coming along, too." Mrs. Greenleaf was an elderly woman the PTs had helped a few months earlier.

Then Miss Kotter handed out a get-well card for everyone to sign for Mrs. Ryan.

Sara was glad the homeless woman was doing so well. But she was still worried about her English assignment. During prayer time, she explained her dilemma to Miss Kotter and the class. "I want to stand up for Jesus and write about His birthday," she said. "But if I get a bad grade, that won't look good for Jesus, either."

"It's not always easy standing up for what's right," Miss Kotter replied. Then she told about a very brave aunt named Jehosheba from the Bible.

"Jehosheba knew that if the wicked queen discovered what she was doing, she would be killed," Miss Kotter explained. "But God helped her be courageous and do the right thing, anyway. And He can help us, too."

That afternoon Miss Kotter borrowed the church van so Mrs. Greenleaf's wheelchair would fit inside it along with the kids from the Sunday school class. At the hospital, the girls learned that June Ryan had lost her job when she hurt her back. Then her only daughter died. When she couldn't pay her rent any more because she didn't have a job or anyone to take care of her, she ended up out on the street.

"I'm so grateful to you all!" she cried. "I know you people really love Jesus, because you were willing to help me. But I don't know where I'll go when I get out of here."

"We can take you to the rescue mission shelter," Miss Kotter offered.

"No," Mrs. Greenleaf interrupted. "She's coming home with me. I insist on it! I have lots of room, and I get so lonely by myself. We can help each other, too. That's if it's all right with Mrs. Ryan." Of course, it was.

The next day in English class, everyone had something entertaining or interesting to tell about winter holidays. No one mentioned Christmas. Miss Anderson smiled and said, "Very good" to all of them.

Then it was Sara's turn. She told about Sam and Petie finding June Ryan, and about her pastor and friends getting the sick woman to the hospital. Then she described how her whole class went to visit Mrs. Ryan. She ended the story by telling about Mrs. Greenleaf's invitation to Mrs. Ryan to live with her.

Miss Anderson frowned. "That's all very nice, Sara. But what does any of that have to do with a winter holiday?"

All eyes were on Sara. Suddenly she was very nervous. Then she remembered Sunday's Bible verse: "Be strong in the Lord and in His mighty power."

"Because Jesus is the one who helped everyone show that love to Mrs. Ryan," she explained. "That's why I'm so glad God sent His Son Jesus to be born on that first Christmas night. That's why Christmas is my favorite holiday. Not because of presents, but because of God's great love."

As she returned to her seat, Sara smiled. No matter what grade her teacher gave her, she already felt like a winner!

· Good News · from God's Word

This is the story that inspired Sara to find courage.

Jehosheba's Daring Rescue

FROM 2 CHRONICLES 22:10-23:11

Queen Athaliah was very, very wicked! When her son Ahaziah became king, she taught him every bad thing she could.

Then one day King Ahaziah was killed. Now his mother was very angry. If her son couldn't rule Judah, then she'd rule it herself. Just to make sure, she ordered everyone else in the royal family to be killed, including her grandson Joash, who was only a year old! Everyone was afraid of this terrible queen. But some people refused to obey her. One of those brave people was King Ahaziah's own sister, Jehosheba. Jehosheba's husband was Jehoida, the priest in charge of the temple. Jehosheba hid baby Joash and his babysitter in the temple for six long years. When Joash was 7 years old, Jehoida and his friends had Joash crowned the new king of God's people.

Jehosheba was glad for the courage to do what was right!

A Verse to Remember

*Be strong in the Lord and
in his mighty power.*

— *Ephesians 6:10*

What About You?

Is there something you're afraid of, such as
the dark, getting F's, becoming sick or being
in an elevator? If so, what is it?

_____

Have you talked to anyone about this fear, such as
your parents, a teacher or your pastor? ____

If not, why not?

_____

_____

If so, what did they tell you?

_____

_____

Sometimes we can help ourselves with our
fears. Afraid of heights? Make sure you stay back from
the edge of a roof. Or don't go all the way up a ladder.
Afraid of tests? Study well, take a deep breath and
make sure you have sharpened pencils. Check out the
activity on the next page for something else that will
help you!

You're a Superhero!

Superheroes are brave. You can be, too. Use the following code to discover how you can find courage to do what's right, even when it's difficult. Write the letters on the lines below the code. The answer is on page 201.

Secret Code

A = 26   B = 25   C = 24   D = 23   E = 22

F = 21   G = 20   H = 19   I = 18   J = 17

K = 16   L = 15   M = 14   N = 13   O = 12

P = 11   Q = 10   R = 9   S = 8   T = 7

U = 6   V = 5   W = 4   X = 3   Y = 2

Z = 1

The Secret to Courage:

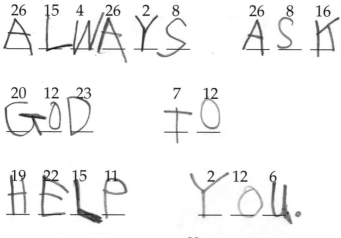

26 15 4 26 2 8   26 8 16
A L W A Y S   A S K

20 12 23   7 12
G O D   T O

19 22 15 11   2 12 6
H E L P   Y O U.

A Promise to Yourself

Write what you're afraid of again on the line below. Then pray and ask God to help you overcome that fear. Sign your name and today's date afterward.

_____

_____

Name _____

Date _____

Advent Calendar

Here is a picture to cut out or copy and paste in the Day 2 square on your Advent calendar. This is an Old Testament scroll, the kind of books people had in Bible times. In God's Word, He promised His people He would send a Savior, but meanwhile they had to have a lot of courage to follow God, just like we do today. The Secret Letter for Chapter 2 is "C" for "Courageous." Write it on line 6.

Chapter 3

Oh, No!
There Goes
Christmas!

Sam and Petie sat on the living room floor admiring their new Christmas tree. It had been fun to put it up — even if their little dog, Sneezit, made a mess of some of the decorations!

The evening news blared away on the TV. "In business today," said the newscaster, "the Friendly Oil Company chain announced that it has just been bought by Interstate Oil, effective immediately."

"Did you hear that, Sam?" Petie said. "That's Dad's company. That means he's getting a new boss."

For years, their father had worked at a Friendly Oil gas station as an auto mechanic. "Maybe he'll get a raise," Sam answered. "Even a Christmas bonus. Wouldn't that be great?"

"Yeah! I need a new bike. I'm tired of riding your old one."

His sister grinned. "And I'd like ballet lessons and a chance to go to basketball camp up at the college. Plus we need a new car, maybe a van or a SUV. A red one would be great. Dad's worked for Friendly for so many years, maybe he'll even get a promotion out of this."

A few minutes later her PTs LaToya and Le came over. "We've got the plans all made for the Zone 56 Christmas caroling tomorrow night, Sam," Le said as she handed Sam a sheet of paper. "Here are the carols we've picked out. If it's not snowing, LaToya's going to bring her guitar along and I'll bring my violin. Pastor Andy's going to lead the singing. Is it still OK to have everyone come back here for snacks afterward?"

"Sure. Mom said we can have hot chocolate and spiced cider and cookies. Maria's mother's bringing over some of her great burritos. I'll ask Mom if we can order pizza, too."

The next day when Sam came home from school, she was surprised to find her mom already home from her job at the animal shelter. But something was even stranger: her dad was already home, too! They were sitting at the kitchen table, and neither one was smiling.

Sam ran in and hugged them both. "Hi, Mom. Hi, Dad. I'm starving. Oh, Mom, can you order some pizzas for tonight, with extra cheese and pepperoni? We need more than just cookies to feed the Zone 56 group."

"Please sit down, Sam," her mom said. "Your dad has something to tell you about his work."

Sam grinned. "Oh, yeah, I heard about it on the news last night. Interstate bought your company out. Do you get a promotion out of it, Dad?"

Her parents looked at each other. When Sam's mom turned her head, Sam could see that her mother had been crying.

Mr. Pearson put his arm around Sam. His eyes were red, too. "No, sweetie. What they didn't say on the news was that Interstate would be closing down most of the Friendly stations and getting rid of all their car repair shops."

"Sam," her mom said quietly, "your father is out of work as of today. We're going to have to be very careful with money around here. I don't make that much at the animal shelter, you know. So, no, we can't order pizza for tonight. And we'll all have to be very understanding about Christmas presents this year."

Sam could hardly believe it. How could God do this to her family? They loved Him; He loved them. It didn't make sense.

Then she remembered the Bible verse: "We know that in all things God works for the good of those who love him." But that didn't make sense, either. All things? Even her father being out of a job? Even with her Christmas suddenly becoming practically impossible?

A big group of Zone 56 members showed up at the church to go caroling. Up and down the snowy streets they went, singing and laughing. They sang "Hark! the Herald Angels Sing," "O Come, All Ye Faithful," "Away in a Manger" and all the rest. Everyone had fun telling about Jesus.

At least, it was fun for everyone but Sam. All she could think about was her dad being out of work. What would her family do now? What could they do?

Then she listened to the words she was singing. This wasn't just anyone's birthday. This was "Christ the Lord," "little Lord Jesus," "the King of Angels." This was the Son of God! Able to do anything to help her!

Sam looked up at the stars as the music surrounded her. "I believe You, dear God," she said. "I believe You love me. And somehow You'll help us through this."

Suddenly she felt a lot better. Hey, who needed pizza anyway, when they could eat some of Mrs. Moreno's delicious burritos!

· Good News · from God's Word

This is the story of a Bible woman who believed God even when times were tough.

Deborah's Victory

FROM JUDGES 4:4-24

Deborah was a very wise woman. She was a very loving one, too. Although she was a busy wife and mother, she also took time to be a teacher and a judge. In addition, she was a prophetess who spoke

God's Word to His people. And she was a musician!

This was not a happy time for Israel. Jabin, king of Canaan, kept making trouble for God's people. He had a huge army with 900 iron chariots and powerful horses. Sisera was his general. Israel had no chariots and no horses. And no general, either!

Then God told Deborah what to do. "Barak," she told one of the men, "God wants you to take 10,000 men up Mount Tabor. General Sisera will come to attack you along the River Kishon. And you will win!"

Barak was scared. He wasn't a general. 10,000 soldiers? He didn't have a single one! And he didn't have any horses and chariots with which to fight. Besides, Mount Tabor was steep and high!

But Barak wanted to do what was right. "I'll go if you go with me, Deborah," he said.

Deborah wasn't a general, either. But she believed God. "I'll go with you," she said. And they did get 10,000 men to fight for God! And they did win! All because Deborah believed God's Word.

 A Verse to Remember

We know that in all things God works for the good of those who love him.

— ***Romans 8:28***

What About You?

The memory verse is shown below, but with a blank space in it. If you really believe God loves you enough to take care of you even in hard times, write your own name in the space.

We know that in all things God works for the good of

_____ who love[s] him.

— Romans 8:28

Here We Go A-Caroling!

How well you do you know the titles of Christmas carols? Select a word from the column on the right to complete each title on the left. Check your answers on page 201. Then test your song sense by singing the first verse of each carol out loud!

1. "Away in a _____"   a. Sing

2. "Silent Night! _____ Night!"   b. Midnight

3. "_____ to the World!"   c. Noel

4. "Angels from the Realms of _____" d. Manger

5. "O Come, All ____ Faithful"   e. Joy

6. "Angels We Have _____ on High"   f. Glory

7. "It Came Upon a _____ Clear"   g. Holy

continued on next page…

8. "Hark! the Herald Angels _____"   h. Ye

9. "The First _____"   i. Little

10. "O _____ Town of Bethlehem"   j. Heard

Have Your Own Carol Night

Whether your streets are lined with snow banks or palm trees at Christmastime, you and your friends can have a great time Christmas caroling. You can go to a shopping center or nursing home, or a safe neighborhood. Here are a few tips for joyful caroling:

1. Who do you want to carol with you? Your family, other kids on your street, your Ponytail Girls club, your Sunday school class or your church youth group are all good ideas.

2. Where will you carol and when? If your site is a hospital or shopping center, be sure to get permission from someone in authority there.

3. Will you sing with instruments? Make sure your time and place are appropriate for instruments if you plan to use them. It's hard to play an accordion while plowing through a tall snow bank!

4. Who will lead the singing to make sure everyone starts on the same note? You don't want to get doors slammed in your face!

5. Will one or more adults be along? This is usually safer, and essential if you need to be driven.

6. What will you sing? If you will be indoors or outside during daylight, you can use song sheets or books. Outdoors at night, sing only a few songs for which everyone knows the first verse. Check out the "Here We Go A-Caroling" quiz above for ideas. Agree on the songs ahead of time with your group.

7. Take flashlights for safety if you go at night.

8. Make arrangements ahead of time for a fun get-together after caroling.

Party Time!

Your carolers will be hungry and thirsty, which is a great excuse for a post-caroling party! For drinks, serve something steaming hot, like tea, spiced cider or cocoa. You can use hot water from a teapot with packages of tea bags, or ready-made cider or cocoa mixes. Provide small candy canes to stick in the tea or cocoa for a special, Christmasy taste. Serve your hot beverages with Christmas cookies, or make the Gingerbread Girls using the recipe on the next page. Be sure to get an adult to help you when using the oven.

Gingerbread Girls

What You Need

- ½ cup butter
- ½ cup white or brown sugar
- ½ cup dark molasses
- 3½ cups all-purpose flour
- 1 teaspoon baking soda
- ¼ teaspoon ground cloves
- ½ teaspoon cinnamon
- 2 teaspoons ginger
- ½ teaspoon salt
- heavy paper or cardboard

What to Do

1. Preheat the oven to 350°.

2. Grease a cookie sheet.

3. Blend the butter and sugar until creamy.

4. Beat in the molasses. Set aside.

5. Sift the flour.

6. Add the baking soda, cloves, cinnamon, ginger and salt to the flour and resift.

7. Gradually add the dry mixture to the butter mixture. Also add ¼ cup of water and mix until blended.

8. Separate the dough into eight sections.

9. Fold in half a sheet of heavy paper or cardboard.

10. Draw an outline for half of a girl (head,

outstretched arm, skirt, leg) so that the front of the girl is along the fold.

11. Open the sheet for a full pattern.

12. Use a rolling pin to roll the dough out on the greased cookie sheet. Roll it thin enough to make eight girls.

13. Place the pattern over the dough and cut around it with the edge of a knife. Mold the extra dough scraps together and roll them out again to cut more girls.

14. Press each Gingerbread Girl flat on a greased cookie sheet.

15. Decorate the Girls with small raisins, candies or bits of candied fruit.

16. Bake the cookies for about 8 minutes or until they spring back when they are touched. Allow them to cool, then decorate them with icing, if you want.

Advent Calendar

Cut out or copy these praying hands and paste them onto the Day 3 square on your Advent calendar. Praying hands remind us how God's people believed His promises and prayed for Him to send His Son, Jesus. The Secret Letter for Chapter 3 is "B" for "believing." Write it on line 14.

Chapter 4

Deck the Halls and Let's Be Jolly

The next morning, the Pearsons' kitchen table was so full of newspapers that Sam could barely find a place to set her cereal bowl. Her father was deep into reading the classified ads. "Find anything interesting?" she asked.

Mr. Pearson set down the paper. He tried to smile, but he had big circles under his eyes. "Sure, sweetie. Now don't you worry about a thing. As long as people drive cars, trucks and tractors, they will need a good mechanic. I'm going to apply all over town. The next county, too, if necessary. But because it's Christmas, finding a new job may take longer than we want."

Sam kissed her dad on the cheek. "You're not just a good mechanic, Dad, you're the very best. I'll be praying for you."

"Me, too," echoed her little brother through a mouthful of corn flakes.

On the way to school, Sam told her PT Maria about her father being out of work.

"I remember last summer when my Papa was out of work," Maria said. "We had to sell our house and move here to Circleville for his new job. But now that we're here, we love it!"

"Oh, I don't want to move anywhere else!" Sam said. "Let's pray that he finds a new job right here in Circleville!"

That day at school, Sara, Le and LaToya all promised to pray about a job for Sam's father. "Let's also pray for Mrs. Ryan," LaToya added, "so that she'll get well enough to live with Mrs. Greenleaf."

"I've got an idea!" Le said suddenly. "Let's put up a Christmas tree at Mrs. Greenleaf's home for them. And maybe one for the people at Whispering Pines. I mean, if we can afford it." The other girls nodded. Whispering Pines was where Miss Kotter's elderly friend, Ma Jones, lived. Everyone loved to visit her.

After school, all five PTs stopped by the Christmas tree lot. Some signs said "pine," some "fir," others "cedar" and "spruce." There were all sizes and prices. "It's too confusing," Sam sighed.

"We need help," Sara decided. "I'll ask one of the workers. Oh, sir, could…"

Then all of their mouths flew open. The worker was Sam's dad! God had certainly answered their prayers for him to get a job. But this wasn't the kind of job Sam had in mind!

He smiled, but he looked embarrassed. "Hello, girls. Can I help you?"

"Hi, Mr. Pearson," LaToya answered without missing a beat. "We're looking for Christmas trees for Mrs. Greenleaf and for the nursing home, too. But we don't have much money. Are there any scraggly ones we could get cheap, or maybe even free?"

He shook his head. "Sorry, girls. My new boss, Mr. Moore, is very strict. He says no price reductions 'til Christmas Eve. And no giveaways 'til after Christmas!"

"Oh, no!" the girls said in unison.

Then he pointed to the ground. "But see all these extra evergreen branches lying around? We have to cut them off for the trees to fit in people's stands. You can have all the branches you want for free. In fact, if you'll take them away, Mr. Moore will pay you $5."

"But what good are the branches by themselves?" Sam asked.

Le pointed at all the evergreen wreaths and swags on display. "For that!" she exclaimed. "We'll take all the branches and decorate with them!"

After letting their parents know where they were, the girls called Miss Kotter at her office. When she stopped by after work, they had a huge pile of evergreen boughs ready to load into her car, plus two trash bags full of sweepings to throw away.

"This is great!" she said. "Why don't we invite all your Zone 56 group to join us? Everyone can bring some ornaments or tinsel to decorate the branches."

The next day, Mrs. Ryan got to leave the hospital and go live with Mrs. Greenleaf. The two elderly women were thrilled for the young people to decorate their porch and living room. Even though Mrs. Greenleaf could hardly see, she could touch and smell the evergreens. "They are just beautiful!" she sighed.

At Whispering Pines, the residents who were able helped the Zone 56 members decorate the rooms. Then everyone sang Christmas carols as LaToya played on her guitar.

That night, Sam prayed, "Dear God, I don't

know why you let Dad lose his job. But thank You for the one he has right now. And thank You so much for loving us all. In Jesus' Name. Amen."

· Good News · from God's Word

When Sam and her friends shared Christmas joy with some elderly people, they all had a wonderful time. Read on to find out what this woman shared with her friends and neighbors.

A Samaritan Woman Sharing Her Joy

FROM JOHN 4:1-42

One day as Jesus and his friends were walking along, it was lunchtime. They were very hungry and thirsty. While Jesus' friends went to buy some lunch, Jesus sat by a well to rest.

Soon a woman came along carrying a big jug. The village women usually went to the well to get water early in the morning. But this woman was ashamed to be around the other women. She had done too many wrong things in her life. That's why she was here at noon.

As she filled her jug, Jesus asked for a drink. "How can you ask me for a drink?" she replied. "You're a Jew and I'm a Samaritan. Jews aren't supposed to talk to Samaritans."

But Jesus loved this woman, just as He loved everyone. Soon He was telling her all about her past. She didn't know what to think about that. Jesus had never seen her before. How did He know all this about her?

"I see that You are a prophet," she said. "Well, when the Messiah comes, He'll tell us everything!"

"I'm the Messiah," Jesus told her. Oh, was she happy to hear that! That instant, she set down her water jug and ran to town. "Come see the Messiah!" she yelled.

They came running. When they met Jesus, they were so thrilled that they asked Him to stay in their town and teach them. Soon many, many people believed in God's Son. How happy they were!

A Verse to Remember

*For God so loved the world that
he gave his one and only Son.*

— John 3:16

What About You?

God loves you so much! Here is the Bible verse again. Write your name in the blank.

For God so loved _____ that
he gave his one and only Son.

— John 3:16

Have you thanked Him? Do so right now. Jesus' birth is the real joy of Christmas!

Decking the Halls

"Decking" means "decorating." Christmas is a wonderful time to help your parents decorate your home. Even if you live in a tiny apartment, you can put a tiny tree on a dresser or table. Or paint a picture of one and tape it to your refrigerator!

O Christmas Tree!

On the next page is a dot-to-dot Christmas tree for you to draw and decorate. See all the ornaments on it? Some of them have letters on them. Write in the rest of the letters, starting at the top, to read "Jesus, God's Christmas Gift of Love." Then finish decorating the picture with crayons, markers or stickers. Draw presents under the tree, too!

Caring Coupons

The most important gift you can give is love. Remember, love is the one Christmas gift that is always appreciated. In fact, it lasts forever!

Caring Coupons are one way to show your love — and they're free! Copy the samples on the next page or make your own. Be sure to write on each coupon what it is for, such as "10 hours of babysitting" or "wash windows" or "read your favorite book to you." But don't give coupons for things that are already regular chores for you!

After decorating each coupon with crayons, markers or stickers, cut them out and put them inside an envelope with the recipient's name on the front. You can also give Caring Coupons at other times of year, such as birthdays.

Advent Calendar

Cut out or copy Mary and glue her on the Day 4 square on the Advent calendar. Like other people in Bible times, Mary prayed that God would send the Savior. But she didn't know that she would be part of God's plan to provide Him! The Secret Letter for Chapter 4 is "S" for "sharing." Write it on line 13.

Merry Christmas

This Caring Coupon
can be redeemed for:

_____

_____

_____
signed

"God is Love"

Merry Christmas

This Caring Coupon
can be redeemed for:

_____

_____

_____
signed

"God is Love"

Chapter 5

From Hoop to Hope

When Sam met Sara after cheerleading practice, Sara's blue eyes had the blues — the sad kind.

"Is Brittany bugging you again?" Sam asked. During the fall, Sara had made cheerleader on the Madison Middle School squad. But somehow

Brittany, the head cheerleader, always found a way to keep Sara from performing. "She's just jealous of you, Sara. Don't let her get you down."

"Yeah, Brittany did it again. Tomorrow's the last game before Christmas vacation, but she wants the squad to do the pyramid — the one stunt I'm not needed on. It's not fair."

Sam sighed. "Well, don't lose hope. That's what I keep telling Dad. He's put in job applications all over town. But only stores seem to hire at Christmas. He's not making much money at the tree lot. At least Grandma and Grandpa Pearson are coming to see us. We'll just have to count that as our Christmas gift this year, I guess."

News always traveled fast at Madison Middle School, and the next day the big news was all about Brittany Boorsma. Not because she was there, but because she wasn't. She was sick in bed with the flu. Sara would have to take her place at the game!

"I'm glad and sad at the same time!" Sara told LaToya when they met in the cafeteria at lunch. "Glad to get to cheer. Sad because I never got to practice what we'll be doing. I know the words, of course. But what if I stumble or fall? Or my glasses fall off, so I can't see?"

LaToya gave her a hug. "Do your best! Don't give up hope! We'll all be rooting for you."

Before the big game that evening, Sara was so nervous she wanted to back out. She kept going over all the cheers in her mind, like "Madison, Madison, you're the one; Madison, Madison, you've got 'em on the run!" And "Madison in Circleville, don't go around the hill. Don't hit the road again. Just play the game and win, win, win!"

When she told the other girls how nervous she was, they all hugged her. "Don't worry," they said. "You'll be great!"

Sara prayed to herself. *Dear God*, she said, *please help me and use me.* Then she waved to her parents in the bleachers and they waved back. Her big brother, Tony, gave her a thumbs-up. Then the game started!

From then on, the evening was a whirl of activity. Back and forth went the players, from one end of the floor to the other, their shorts and shirts a blur of color. The ball was everywhere, too — basket after basket. Madison had never played so well, but the other team was just as good.

The band played and played. Everyone clapped. The cheerleaders never stopped.

What a night! Madison even won! All of Sara's friends and family praised her work.

"You were good," said Jennifer, one of the other cheerleaders, as she threw an arm around Sara to hug her. "Who needs Miss Uppity Brittany? Forget her."

But Sara couldn't forget Brittany, even though she had been so mean to Sara all fall. She asked the team and the squad to sign a basketball for Brittany. At home, Mrs. Fields helped Sara decorate a pot of red Christmas poinsettias. Then she and Jennifer took the ball and flowers to Brittany's house.

Brittany was too sick to see the girls, but her mother thanked them. The next day Sara got a call. It was Brittany.

"Thanks for the flowers and ball," she croaked through a very sore throat. "I hear you did a good job with the squad last night."

"Not as good as you do, Brittany," Sara replied, even though it was difficult to admit it. "Everyone missed you. We're all sorry you're sick. I hope you feel better soon."

Brittany was quiet for a minute. Then she said, "Thanks, Sara. For everything. I know I haven't been very nice to you lately, but I'll try to do better. OK?"

"Sure. Just get well so you can have fun at Christmas." When Sara hung up the phone she was so happy, she turned a cartwheel right down the hallway!

· Good News · from God's Word

Do you know someone like Brittany who needs to hear about God? That's the situation Rahab was in long ago in Jericho. Read on.

Rahab's Decision for God

FROM JOSHUA 2, 6

All her life Rahab had heard about God's people, the Israelites. God had always taken care of them. He helped them cross the Red Sea and He fought for them against cruel kings. Her own people worshipped cruel idols, but Rahab wanted very much to worship and honor God. Yet how could she do it without someone's help?

Rahab's hometown was Jericho, a large city by the Jordan River. Jericho was a very old, very busy city surrounded by a huge wall. No enemies could conquer the city because the wall was so strong.

God's people had been in Egypt for hundreds of years. Now they were ready to come back to Israel. That meant crossing over the Jordan River without the soldiers of Jericho capturing them! So two of the Israelites visited the city to look it over. Rahab invited them to stay at her house overnight. She had to pretend they weren't there so they wouldn't be killed.

That night she told them, "The Lord your God is God in heaven above and on the earth below. I believe that God will let your people conquer my city. When that happens, please spare my parents and brothers and sisters and relatives."

They promised to do so. The next morning Rahab dropped a red rope from her upstairs window for them to use as an escape. "Keep the rope tied in your window," they said. "That way we'll know which house is yours so we can save you."

The men kept their promise. When God made the great walls fall, the Israelites rescued Rahab and her family. She became a great believer in the Lord. In fact, she married and became one of Jesus' ancestors!

A Verse to Remember

We have put our hope in the living God.
— *1 Timothy 4:10*

What About You?

Think of someone you really don't like. Maybe he or she has said mean things about you. Hurtful things. Even lies. Maybe you were snubbed or made fun of or bullied. Maybe this person has always been favored by your teachers over you, no matter how hard you try. Maybe you can't even see or remember that person without thinking angry thoughts. If so, write that person's name here:

_____

The trouble with hate is that it hurts you a lot more than the person you don't like. God tells us to love others, including our enemies. Pray right now and ask God to help you think about doing good for Him instead of doing bad to others. Even pray that the person you don't like will turn to God and change. Then write today's date: _____

However, if you don't like someone, especially an adult, because that person has hurt you physically or made you do something wrong, you need to tell your parents, your pastor or a teacher as soon as possible.

Advent Calendar

Cut out or copy the angel Gabriel and glue it onto the Day 5 square on your Advent calendar. The angel Gabriel was sent by God to Mary to tell her about baby Jesus. The Secret Letter for chapter 5 is "S" for "steadfast." Write it on line 3.

Let's Hear a Cheer

Sara's all ready to cheer. On the next page, make her outfit match your own school's colors and draw the first letter of your school on her sweater.

Chapter 6

Joy to the World!

The last Friday afternoon before Christmas vacation, the Madison Middle School's choirs and bands gave their annual winter concert for the other students, teachers and staff.

Sam and Maria sang with the Girls' Chorus. Le played a violin solo. LaToya and her beloved Granny B. did a duet on "I Wonder as I Wander," along with the Jazz Choir. Everyone clapped along to "Winter Wonderland" with Kevin Hickory on the drums and

Sam Schneider on the bass guitar.

Jenna Jenkins grinned afterward to Sam as she hung up her choir robe. Jenna was tall like Maria, but willowy. A ballet student, she wore her light brown hair in a high ponytail almost like a crown. Jenna had been coming to the Zone 56 group for a couple of months. But she didn't come to Sunday school yet.

"Wasn't that a great concert?" Jenna exclaimed. "I love Christmas music!"

"Yes," Sam replied, "but I wish more of the songs had been real Christmas ones about Jesus, instead of just winter or Santa Claus. Remember how fun the Zone 56 caroling party was?"

Jenna nodded, then turned to Le, "I loved your violin solo, Le. Are you doing any more concerts this Christmas?"

Le sighed. "Yes, unfortunately, tonight. Mom and I are playing for a Vietnamese church's Christmas sing-along. But I don't really want to. I want to sing in English, not in Vietnamese. But Mom's a new Christian, so I want to encourage her."

"Could I come along?" Jenna asked.

Le stared at her. "I'm not very good at Vietnamese, but you don't know any at all. What will you do?"

Laughing, Maria answered for her. "So she'll sing along in English. Hey, I was telling some other people about this and there's a bunch of us who'd like to come, if that's all right. I know you don't have room for us all in your mom's car, but we can carpool. Maybe Miss Kotter would like to go, too.

What do you think?"

Now it was Le's turn to grin. "That would make it fun for me and Mom!"

When Sam got home that afternoon, she rushed inside. "Mom! Petie!" she called, as she put her dirty gym clothes in the laundry hamper. "I'm home!"

But no one answered. Instead, there was a note by the phone.

Hi, Sam,
Petie came home sick, so I had to take time off from work and get him to the doctor. When we come back, I'll need you to watch him while I go back to the animal shelter and finish up. Please take a frozen casserole out for dinner. Stick it in the oven at 350. Your dad has to work late tonight.
Love, Mom

"No!" Sam cried out loud. "There goes Le's sing-along. I never get to do anything fun!"

Sighing, she called Le to say that she couldn't make it.

"Is this what my whole Christmas vacation is going to be like — work, work, work?" Sam said out loud to herself as she pulled the casserole from the freezer and turned on the oven. "Isn't Christmas supposed to be a time of joy?"

By the time Mrs. Pearson and Petie returned, the casserole was ready. Sam had also set the table and made a salad. But her mother didn't have time to eat, and Petie didn't feel like eating. He took his first dose of medicine and lay down on the couch. Sam turned on the TV for him. Then she served herself and sat down at the kitchen table to eat. By herself.

Just then she heard the beautiful sound of Christmas carols. She couldn't make out the words, but she already knew them by heart, so she started singing along between bites.

"Sam!" her little brother cried suddenly. "Come quick!"

Sam jumped up and ran into the living room. Was he sicker? No, he was pointing at the TV. "Look! There's Le's mom at the piano! And Le, too, with her violin! They're on TV!"

Sam brought her plate into the living room. Then Petie snuggled up to her for the special

Christmas program. She didn't miss the concert, after all! In fact, her mom and dad returned home before it was over, so they got to enjoy it, too.

Yes, Sam thought later as she got ready for bed, *even with sickness and losing jobs and everything, Christmas is still a wonderful time. The very best time in the entire year!*

· Good News ·
from God's Word

Sam discovered something on her TV. Rhoda discovered something joyful at her front door! Read the following story and see if you can guess what she saw.

Rhoda's Glad News

FROM ACTS 12:1-19

Rhoda was worried. Peter had been captured and thrown into jail just because he preached about Jesus. Now wicked King Herod had 16 soldiers guarding him. He planned to beat Peter up…maybe even kill him!

That night Peter slept at the jail, chained to two guards. But the other Christians weren't sleeping.

They were all at Mark's mother's house, praying for Peter. Young Rhoda, a servant girl, kept watch at the door to make sure they didn't all get captured, too.

Meanwhile at the jail, an angel suddenly appeared. He woke Peter. "Get up!" the angel said. Then the chains fell right off of Peter and the angel led him outside. He was free!

Soon the Christians who were praying together heard a knock at the door. "I'll get it," Rhoda said. At the door she called, "Who is it?"

"Peter," came the answer.

"Peter?" Rhoda was so excited, she completely forgot to open the door. Instead, she ran and told everyone. "It's Peter!" she shouted.

"No," they said. "That's impossible. You're imagining things."

Poor Peter kept knocking away. Finally, they came to let him in. What joy! Everyone started talking at the same time. And Rhoda was happiest of all!

 ## A Verse to Remember

Praise the Lord, for the Lord is good.

— *Psalm 135:3*

What About You?

What was the happiest time in your life?
Write about it here:

_____

_____

Did you tell God "thank You" for that happy time? If
no, tell Him now and write today's date here:

_____

What you can do to help someone else have a happy
day? Write it here:

_____

_____

Advent Calendar

Cut out or copy and glue Elizabeth
on the Day 6 square on your Advent
calendar. Mary's relative Elizabeth welcomed her.
Elizabeth was John the Baptist's mother. The Secret
Letter for chapter 6 is "J" for "joyful." Write it on line 1.

Rhoda's Praise Maze

Help Peter find his way from the jail to Mark's
mother's house and safety. Notice Rhoda is there to
welcome him! The solution is on page 202.

start

finish

Chapter 7

Oh, No, Not Suzie!

Sam stared at the calendar. Now that Christmas vacation had started, she had just a little over a week to do her Christmas shopping. But first she had to find some money to do it with! She still had the $5 that her Grandma Pearson had sent her. But there was no way she could buy for everyone with that!

Sam called the PTs together. "I need a

babysitting job," she said.

"We all do," replied LaToya.

"Trouble is, Sam," Maria added, "you already have to babysit Petie for free. And I already have to babysit the twins and Lolita. How can you and I babysit anyone else?"

Sara snapped her fingers. "I have an idea. What about something like a camp for kids during Christmas break? The older kids could do fun things together and maybe Granny B. could help us with the younger ones. Even though she's in a wheelchair, they like her stories and she can rock them to sleep. I think Tony's free this vacation, too. I'll see if he can help us out with games."

"My mom's off this week, too," LaToya remembered. "Since she's a teacher she'll have good ideas for things to do with kids. I could even ask my sister, Tina, to give us some first aid training."

Sam started writing down their ideas. "We need to advertise, figure out what we'll need and get permission slips and phone numbers from all the parents who sign up. What if we charge $5 for each morning or afternoon, including snacks; $10 for all day including lunch; and $7 for any evening up 'til 11:00? Besides people at church and neighbors, can you think of anyone else we should tell?"

"What about your cousin Suzie, Sam?" Le asked.

Sam pretended to gag. "Oh, no! Not Suzie! Not my bratty little cousin!" She reminded them about the time last summer when Suzie almost drowned because she wouldn't listen to anyone. "I want our camp to be fun, not full of whiners like Suzie."

The PTs told their parents their plan and their parents all agreed to it. The camp would be held every day at LaToya's house, with Mrs. Thomas and Granny B. supervising. Mrs. Moreno would come over and help, too. So would Sara's big brother, Tony. Mrs. Pearson made a list of safety rules for everyone to follow. Miss Kotter loaned them a stack of kids' Christian videos.

But the PTs were responsible for planning all the activities. "And no just setting the children down in front of the TV for cartoons!" all their mothers warned.

The PTs prayed together to ask God's help in making the week a blessing for everyone. Then they made fliers and passed them out to everyone they could think of. By Sunday afternoon, six children had been signed up for each afternoon of the following week. Seven more parents reserved times so they could shop or go to parties. Two little tots needed care each morning. And that was in addition to Maria's little brothers and sister and Petie!

"Well," laughed Granny B. when she heard the news. "Looks as though we all have our hands full!"

Later at home, Sam got out her calculator and added up how much money they would make. A lot! Then she divided that total among all the girls who would be working. Suddenly it wasn't very much.

We need some kids to take care of who'll be here all day every day, Sam decided. *But how will we find any like that?*

Just then, Sam's Aunt Caitlin called. Suzie's mother! "Sam, honey," she said, "I hear you and your friends are babysitting for people during your vacation."

Sam gulped. "Uh, yes, Aunt Caitlin."

"Perfect! My sister Candy has asked me to help her out this week at her pet store. I know you girls are charging $50 for the week. I may have to go in earlier some days or work later on others, so how about if I pay $75? I could really use the help."

Sam wanted to say "no." But the word wouldn't come out. After all, she had been praying for years for Aunt Caitlin and Uncle Todd to become Christians. Maybe this would be a way to show them Jesus' love. "Sure, Aunt Caitlin. See you at Mrs. Thomas' in the morning."

When Sara heard about it, she said, "$75! That's great!"

"Don't worry," Sam replied grimly. "We'll be earning it watching Suzie!"

That night at the Zone 56 meeting, when Sam told about the Christmas Kids Camp, Jenna was excited. "My little sister, Katie, and I would love to be a part of your camp," she said. "Mom could help with snacks and lunches. She bakes the best cookies! And I could bring over Katie's picture books and toys to share."

"But your mother is expecting her baby soon, Jenna," Sara protested. "Is she up to helping?"

"Oh, yeah, I think so. She just said the other day that she's never felt better in her life."

So Monday morning the PTs, plus Jenna, reported for camp duty at LaToya's house. Six children did, too, including Petie; Maria's little brothers, Ricardo and Juan, and her little sister, Lolita; Jenna's little sister, Katie; and Suzie. Plus two babies too young to walk and a playful collie named Scott, whom the PTs had agreed to "dogsit." Also there were LaToya's big sister, Tina, a nursing student; her mother and her grandmother, Granny B. What a houseful!

While the boys played with blocks and toy cars, the three girls played doll house. Granny B. watched them while Tina gave the PTs a short class on first aid. "It's good to know what to do in case of an emergency," Tina said at the end of the lesson. "It's even better to prevent an emergency if you can." Then she left for her job at the mall.

As the babies napped, Granny B. told the older children a story. LaToya led them in some Christmas songs. For lunch, Jenna's mom brought over sandwiches, milk, cookies and apples.

"How are you doing, dear?" Mrs. Thomas asked Mrs. Jenkins. "When is your baby due?"

"Not 'til February, believe it or not," Mrs. Jenkins said with a laugh as she smoothed her blouse over her large belly. "But it's not just one baby. It's twins!"

Mrs. Thomas, smiling, gave an exaggerated sigh. "Congratulations! Oh, goodness, you are going to have your hands full soon!"

That afternoon, parents picked up the smaller babies, then six more children were dropped off. Tony played dodge ball with the older children in the basement. Then came quiet time with puzzles or crayons and coloring books. Afterward, Mrs. Moreno came by to tell a Bible story.

"All right, kids," Sam said, "let's put away the toys now. It's story time."

"No!" Suzie yelled. "I'm not done yet."

Sam tried to reason with her, but Suzie got angrier and angrier. Soon she was sobbing at the top of her lungs. She kicked her feet and pounded her fists. Her breath came in big gulps and her face turned red. Some of the other children started crying, too. Others giggled.

"Time out, Suzie," Granny B. said. She picked up Suzie and held her tightly on her lap. At first, Suzie kicked and tried to push away. But then Granny B. started singing, "Jesus Loves Me." LaToya played along on her guitar. The PTs sang, too. And soon the other children began joining in.

As Suzie quieted down, Mrs. Moreno began the Bible story. She told how long ago Moses moved to a new land. "In his old land he was a rich, famous prince. In the new land, though, he was a poor stranger. How lonely he was! Maybe scared, too. Have you ever been scared?"

"I've been scared," Suzie whispered. "I was scared to come today. I wanted to stay home with Mommy and my cat, Precious. I was afraid I wouldn't know any of the kids. I was afraid they wouldn't want to share. But mostly I was afraid Sam didn't like me any more."

Sam was so ashamed to hear her say that. She didn't know that little Suzie actually realized she didn't want her there.

Mrs. Moreno smiled. "And see, God took care of you just as He took care of Moses. In fact, He gave Moses lots of new friends. Just as God has given you a lot of new friends today."

Granny B. gave Suzie a tissue. Suzie dried her eyes and blew her nose. Then she smiled. "I like having friends," she said as she plopped down next to Lolita and Katie. "And I like God, too!"

· Good News · from God's Word

This is the story Mrs. Moreno told the children.

Zipporah's Loving Help
FROM EXODUS 2:15-22

Moses ran away from Egypt because in anger he had killed a man there. Now he was afraid that he would be killed, too. So he ran and ran and ran until he was too tired to run any more. But now he was out in the desert. In some places, he saw nothing but sand. In other places, he saw nothing but mountains. Back in Egypt he had been a rich, famous prince.

Here, he was a poor stranger. He was lonely, scared, hot and thirsty.

Finally Moses came to a well. He took a long drink, then sat down in the shade to rest. While he rested, seven girls came to the well — all sisters. One sister was named Zipporah. The girls had lots and lots of sheep with them. The sheep were hot and thirsty, too. But when they started to give their sheep some water to drink, mean men came and tried to chase them away.

Moses jumped up. "Stop that!" he cried. He chased the men away and helped the girls water their flock. They were so thankful that they ran home and told their father. He was a priest who loved God. He invited Moses home for lunch, then asked if he wanted to stay and live with them. The girls taught Moses how to take care of sheep.

Later, when the girls grew up, Moses married Zipporah. They had two little boys. Moses was glad for this kind, God-loving family. And how glad they were for him! This is the same Moses God called to lead His people to the Promised Land. Zipporah and her father, who obeyed God, helped Him fulfill his plan.

A Verse to Remember

*Whoever claims to live in
him must walk as Jesus did.*

— *1 John 2:6*

What About You?

Have you ever been a babysitter? If so, write below the funniest thing that happened to you when you babysat. If you have not babysat before, write something funny that happened when you were younger and had a babysitter:

_____

_____

Now write the saddest or most embarrassing thing that happened:

_____

_____

Babysitting Like a Pro

Here are the rules the PTs used for their kids' Christmas camp:

1. Always ask God to help you.

2. Know exactly what time and on what day you are to begin babysitting, and what time it will end. Write it on a calendar.

3. Ask where the parents want you to babysit — their home or yours. Write down their address and phone number for you and your parents.

4. Always make sure there is an adult you can reach in an emergency while babysitting — a neighbor, your parents or the child's parents.

5. In life-threatening situations, dial 911 first, then call the parents or another adult.

6. Make sure you have the phone number and address of the place where the child's parents can be reached while you are babysitting, plus their pager or cell phone numbers, if they have them.

7. Make sure the parents know what you charge.

8. Keep all cabinets and drawers closed so a child can't get into them.

continued on next page…

9. Don't let a toddler near stairs or a bathtub alone. Don't let a child near a heater.

10. If you smell smoke, get yourself and the children out of the house first. Then call 911 from a neighbor's house.

11. Never snoop or look through the parents' personal items.

12. If you are allowed to "raid the fridge," make sure you know which items you can eat or drink.

13. Don't make long phone calls.

14. Don't have friends over without permission.

15. At night time, always have a ride home.

16. If you listen to music or watch TV, keep the sound low so you can hear the children.

17. Keep the doors locked. Don't let anyone in except the parents, unless they have told you ahead of time that someone else will be coming.

18. If you have homework to do, wait to do it when the children are asleep.

continued on next page...

19. Don't fall asleep!

20. Do not babysit more than two children at a time without an adult's help until you get older and have more experience with kids.

Babysitting is a big responsibility. If you want to be the best Christian babysitter, check out *The Official Christian Babysitting Guide*. It is full of tips like those you just read, plus it has lots of ideas for Bible-based activities you can do with the kids. Turn to page 208 for more information about *The Official Christian Babysitting Guide*.

Advent Calendar

Cut out or copy and paste Joseph, Jesus' earthly father, onto the Day 7 square on your Advent calendar. This picture shows Joseph praying for God to send His Son, Jesus. The Secret Letter for Chapter 7 is "I" for "imitating Christ." Write it on line 12.

Chapter 8

Don't Go Off
Half-Baked

Everyone loved the cookies Jenna's mother baked for the Christmas camp. "I can bake good cookies, too," Jenna said to the PTs during a break in the camp. "Would you like me to teach you?"

"Yes!" said the other girls, almost in unison. "That way we can make cookies for the rest of this week without bothering your mother."

"And give some away for Christmas gifts, too," Sam added.

That evening after all the camp kids had been picked up, and the PTs had gone home for dinner, they gathered at Sam's house. Jenna, Katie and Lolita came, too. Mrs. Pearson helped the older girls find the flour, sugar, cookie sheets and other supplies in the Pearsons' kitchen they would need. "I love to bake, too," she said. "So if you need me, I'll be in the living room helping Petie and Lolita learn their parts for the Christmas program at church."

Then Jenna showed them some of her mom's cookie recipes. Mrs. Jenkins had written them on little note cards that had "Karen's Kitchen" printed on them with a tea pot and flowers.

"I love those sugar cookies with red and green sprinkles!" LaToya exclaimed. "Yum!"

"Chocolate chips for me," decided Sara. "They just melt in your mouth."

"So do oatmeal cookies with raisins," Sam added. "And they're good for you, not that this is health food time!"

The PTs and Jenna decided to divide into three teams and make all three kinds of cookies.

Soon the counter and sink were full of messy bowls and spoons. But the oven was full of wonderful smells. "This is fun!" Le exclaimed as she started washing the dishes. "Do we get to eat any, too?"

"I want some!" Petie called from the living room.

Just then the phone rang. Sam's mom

answered it. "That was your Grandma Pearson," she told Sam a few minutes later. "They plan to fly out a couple of days before Christmas. They don't want to get snowed in at the last minute like they did at Thanksgiving."

"Yeah!" Petie shouted. "Grandpa can help me build a snow fort."

Just then there was an eeeekkkkkkk followed by a CRASH!

"A car wreck!" everyone yelled as they ran outside. So did many of Sam's neighbors. But the guilty driver gunned his motor and sped off into the dark. No one could see the license plate, but they did see what he had hit: a golden cocker spaniel, which was now lying in the middle of the street.

Mrs. Pearson knelt down by the stricken animal. "He's still breathing!" she cried. "But we need to get him to a vet quickly! Does anyone know whose dog this is?"

Nobody knew, and the dog didn't have tags. "Dr. Grant has an emergency vet clinic," Mrs. Pearson said. "I know him from the animal shelter where I work. We'd better rush him there."

"I have a board in the garage we can slide under him," Mr. Moreno said. "That way we can move him without disturbing any broken bones." Then he and Sam's mom rushed the dog to Dr. Grant's clinic.

Back at Sam's, the girls finished baking a week's supply of cookies. But now instead of saying,

"Umm! How good that looks!" they asked, "How soon do you think your mom will call, Sam?" and "Do you think the dog will live?"

Finally the adults returned. Mr. Moreno looked very sad. "The poor *perro* was hurt very bad," he said.

"Let's pray that we'll find his owners," Mrs. Pearson added. "What a shame that the dog didn't have his ID tags."

"What if we don't find his owners?" Petie asked.

"Yeah," Sara added. "Who's going to pay the doctor bill?"

Suddenly Sam felt awful. As if it weren't bad enough that the dog was hurt, there didn't seem to be anyone who could pay for his care. It would take all of her babysitting money that week and a whole lot more to pay such a bill, she thought. There went Christmas presents again. *Please, God, that's not fair!*

Her mom looked worried. "The pet store where Sam's Aunt Caitlin works might help us. The Paws and Pooches Shelter can probably contribute $50 or so. Dr. Grant will give us a discount, too. But for the rest..."

The girls looked at each other. "We'll all contribute, Mrs. Pearson," Jenna said. "We'll help find his owners, too! We're all one team here, right?"

"Right!" said the others.

Sam gave Jenna a big hug. "Yes, Jenna, one team. Including you. You're a PT, now, too!"

· Good News · from God's Word

Here's how one family worked together as a team to save an entire nation.

Miriam's Teamwork

FROM EX. 2:1-8; 6:20, 26-30; 7:1-6; 14:21-31; 15:1-21

When Miriam was young, she was the big sister of her family. She helped babysit her little brother, Aaron, and her baby brother, Moses. Life was hard in Egypt for her family, who were all slaves. But Miriam loved her family. Because she was a brave and quick thinker, she helped baby Moses to be adopted by a princess, the Pharaoh's daughter. That helped her whole family to live a better life.

Years passed. They all grew up. Moses became a prince in Pharaoh's palace. Miriam and Aaron had regular lives among the people. Maybe they were jealous of him sometimes, but they were proud of him anyway. And he could be proud of them, too. Then one day Moses ran away to the desert. Now he wasn't a prince anymore, but a hard worker just like them. He married and had a family. Years later, God called him to go back to Egypt and lead His people out of slavery.

The two brothers and sister hadn't been together for a long time. By now they were all elderly. But they welcomed Moses home and worked with him to free God's people. Aaron, now a leader among the Israelites, helped Moses speak before the Pharaoh and others. Miriam was a leader among the women. She was also a musician and a prophetess.

How glad they were that God helped them not only to be together again, but to work together as a team for Him!

 ## A Verse to Remember

Join with others in following my example.
— *Philippians 3:17*

What About You?

Have you ever been on a team? If so, what kind?

_____

What was your role on the team? _____

_____

How did being on a team make your task easier?

_____

How did being on a team make your task harder?

_____

If you've never been on a team, do you ever work as
a team with your family? _____

What does your family do as a team?

_____

Does your family work better as a team or not? Why?

_____

How can teamwork honor God?

_____

Oatmeal Raisin Cookies

This is the recipe the PTs used to make Mrs. Jenkins' cookies.

What You Need

- ½ cup butter, softened
- ½ cup firmly-packed brown sugar
- ½ cup granulated sugar
- 1 egg
- 1 t. vanilla
- 1 T. milk
- 1 cup all-purpose flour, sifted
- ½ t. baking soda
- ½ t. double-acting baking powder
- ½ t. salt
- 1 cup uncooked quick oats
- ½ cup raisins

What to Do

1. Preheat oven to 350°.

2. Grease a cookie sheet.

3. Cream ½ cup of butter.

4. Add both sugars to the butter and mix well.

5. Add the egg, vanilla and milk and beat until smooth. Set aside.

continued on next page…

6. Sift together the flour, baking soda, baking powder and salt.

7. Add the dry ingredients to the butter mixture and beat until smooth.

8. Add the oats and raisins. (You can also add coconut or chocolate chips.) Beat well.

9. Drop the dough from a teaspoon about 2" apart on the cookie sheet. Bake 10-15 minutes or until light brown.

Advent Calendar

Cut out or copy Joseph and paste him onto the Day 8 square of your Advent calendar. This picture shows Joseph sleeping. God is talking to him in a dream about baby Jesus. The Secret Letter for chapter 8 is "T" for "team player." Write it on line 11.

Chapter 9

Corn Pops, Car Stops

The next day, the Christmas camp kids
created Christmas cards out of colored paper. Then the
PTs showed them how to make popcorn balls. When
the balls were hard, they wrapped them in brightly-
colored plastic wrap and tied them with ribbons.

"You can give them for presents," Sara said.
"Or hang them on your Christmas tree."

"I want to give mine to one of those grandmas at the Whispering Pines place," Suzie said.

"Me, too!" shouted Juan. "Or to Mrs. Greenleaf."

They strung leftover popcorn into long strings for decorating.

Meanwhile, everyone kept waiting for the phone to ring. "Mom said Dr. Grant would call her at work," Sam explained. "Then she'd call us."

Jenna looked sad enough to cry. "I've been worried about that poor dog all night," she sighed. "I hope he's going to be all right."

When the phone did ring, four girls ran to answer it — along with Scott, the collie! But it was Miss Kotter calling, not Mrs. Pearson.

"Hi, girls," she said. "I just wanted to call and see how you were all doing. I've had a really fun day. I finally got Bob's Christmas presents all wrapped and sent." Bob was Miss Kotter's boyfriend who was overseas in the Navy. "They're going all the way to Australia, you know. Of course, if he's already on his way back to the States it will take him forever to get them. But," she said with a giggle, "it would be more fun having him here with me, anyway!"

The girls told Miss Kotter about the injured dog, and she expressed her sadness, too. Then she added, "I want to thank you girls for helping Lolita and Petie with their parts for the church Christmas program. Could you help with their costumes, too? How about practicing a Christmas carol or two with your camp kids to sing during the program that night?"

Right away, Granny B. found some old towels

and fabric scraps to turn into costumes. Petie was Joseph and Lolita was Mary. Le and LaToya decided to teach the children "Away in a Manger" and "Silent Night." Then they practiced with them.

Finally...*rrrring!*

Mrs. Thomas answered this time. "Yes," she said. "Yes, I see. Yes, I'll tell them." Then she hung up.

"Well?" everyone cried. "What did Sam's mom say?"

"Praise the Lord, kids, that poor little dog is going to make it. That's the good news."

"Yeah!" everyone cheered.

"See, God did answer our prayers!" cried Jenna.

"But the bad news," LaToya's mother continued, "is that Mrs. Pearson's car died on her way to work."

"Oh, no!" Sam cried. "How will she get home? Dad could fix it, but he's got to work late at the tree lot tonight."

"LaToya's dad can pick her up this evening before he goes to work," Mrs. Thomas replied.

"Maria's papa can go along, too" added Mrs. Moreno. "Even though he works as a janitor, he knows a lot about cars. Maybe he can get her car started for her."

"Thanks," Sam said. But inside she felt sad. No one knew as much about cars as her own dad. But now his auto mechanic job was over. And pretty soon his Christmas tree job would be over, too. What would they do then?

"Did Mrs. Pearson say when the dog can come

home?" Jenna asked.

"Yes. Tomorrow. Of course, we don't know where his home is."

"I wish we could keep him," Jenna sighed. "But we can't. Not with my mom about to have twins!"

"He can stay a while at our house," Sam decided. "We already have Sneezit, so we have plenty of dog food. Meanwhile, we'll look for his owners."

"Why don't we all make some posters telling about him?" Suzie asked.

Sam gave her a hug. "Great thinking, Suzie! We can put up posters at church and the shelter and your aunt's pet store. Plus pass out fliers all up and down our street."

And to think, she used to consider her little cousin just a pest!

Soon, little hands were busy hand-printing signs that read:

Lost dog found! Is he yours?

They also wrote Mrs. Thomas' phone number on the posters since that's where they would be most of the week. After the children drew pictures of dogs on their posters, the PTs helped them bundle up to go outside.

"Merry Christmas!" they called to all the neighbors as they distributed the fliers. They even sang Christmas songs as they hurried along the snowy sidewalks. Back at Mrs. Thomas' home, everyone had hot cocoa and some of the girls' freshly-baked cookies.

By the time camp was over for the day and everything was cleaned up, Sam's mom was home. So were Maria's and LaToya's fathers.

"I got her car started," Mr. Moreno said. "But in case that problem happens again, I think I'll walk on down to the tree lot and tell Joe what I did. Oh, and I want show him something, too."

Then he held up a newspaper ad. It read:

```
Wanted: Experienced
auto mechanics to open
new car repair shop.
```

"Yeah!" Petie cried. "Now Dad can get a better job and we can have Christmas after all!"

· Good News · from God's Word

Sometimes it's fun just to do nothing, but not for long. Especially when you're sick!

A Mother-in-Law's Healing

FROM MATTHEW 8:14-17; LUKE 4:38-39

Jesus was so busy! He had been preaching on a mountainside to huge crowds. When He finished, the crowds followed Him everywhere.

"Please heal me!" cried one man.

"Please heal my servant!" cried another.

Jesus healed them both.

As He traveled near the Sea of Galilee, Jesus came to the town of Capernaum. He went into the synagogue. This is where the Jewish people worshipped. Jesus taught them God's Word. He healed a sick person there, too. Everyone was amazed!

Afterward, Jesus went to Simon Peter's house. Peter and his brother Andrew were fishermen. Jesus loved to visit them. He talked with Peter's family about God's Good News. Usually, Peter's mother-in-law enjoyed preparing a good meal for Jesus to eat.

But this time when Jesus came to visit, Peter's mother-in-law didn't have a big meal ready for Him. She didn't even run to tell Him hello. She was sick in bed with a high fever. She felt terrible! She felt even worse that she couldn't show Jesus how much she loved Him. Peter and his wife were worried about her.

But Jesus knew what to do. He healed the sick

woman instantly. And just as instantly, she jumped right up to cook a delicious meal!

A Verse to Remember

Whatever your hand finds to do,
do it with all your might.

— Ecclesiastes 9:10

What About You?

God always answers prayers. But not always the way we expect. Think about the past. Can you remember God answering one of your prayers? If so, write about it here:

_____

_____

_____

_____

_____

_____

Popping Fun

Native Americans have been having fun with popcorn for at least 7000 years. You can, too. The simplest way is to buy microwave popcorn and follow the directions. If you use an electric popper, follow its directions. Or, use this recipe:

What You Need

- heavy skillet or 4-quart pan
- 1 tablespoon vegetable oil
- ½ cup popcorn kernels
- salt
- 2 tablespoons melted butter or margarine (optional)

What to Do

1. Pour the oil in the pan.
2. Add ½ cup popcorn kernels. Cover.
3. Cook over high heat, gently shaking the pan constantly.
4. You might have to hold down the lid when the corn starts popping.
5. When it stops popping, pour the popcorn into a bowl and discard the unpopped kernels.
6. Sprinkle lightly with salt and, if desired, the melted butter or margarine.

Popcorn Balls

What You Need

- 8 cups popped popcorn
- ½ cup sugar
- ¼ cup margarine or butter
- ½ cup light corn syrup
- ⅛ teaspoon salt
- food coloring (if desired)

What to Do

1. Heat all the ingredients except the popcorn to simmering in a large heavy pan or skillet over medium-high heat. Stir constantly.

2. Stir in the popcorn. Continue stirring until the popcorn is well-coated, about 3 minutes.

3. Remove the popcorn from the heat.

4. Dip your hands in cold water.

5. Shape the popcorn into balls.

6. Wrap each ball in plastic wrap.

Note: For caramel balls, substitute brown sugar for regular sugar and dark corn syrup for light. For chocolate balls, add 2 tablespoons of cocoa.

Advent Calendar

Cut out or copy Mary and paste her onto Day 9 on your Advent calendar. This picture shows Mary on her way to Bethlehem where baby Jesus will be born. The Secret Letter for chapter 9 is "I" for "industrious." Write it on line 9.

Chapter 10

Lost...and Found!

For craft projects the following day, the Christmas camp kids made clay-bead and yarn necklaces for gifts. Then the PTs helped them cut star shapes out of gold-colored paper and print "Jesus loves you" on the stars.

When Jenna's mother brought over sandwiches for the children's lunches, she looked pale. "I just feel tired today," she said when Mrs. Thomas showed concern.

"You probably need more rest," Mrs. Thomas replied. "You don't want to come down with a cold right before Christmas. Not with the babies coming!"

"I'll be all right," Mrs. Jenkins insisted. "Thanks for caring. Actually, having Katie over here is helping me a lot." And she went on home.

After she left, Jenna whispered to Mrs. Thomas, "Please pray for Mom. I'm really worried about her."

The next time the front door opened, everyone cheered. It was Mrs. Pearson, carrying the injured dog! The golden cocker spaniel had a lot of bandages on his side, and a cast on one leg. But his tail was wagging.

"Now, kids," Sam's mom said, "don't crowd too close. I just wanted you to see how God answered your prayers."

Maria's little brothers patted the collie's head. "Poor *perro*," they said.

"Perro...that's a good name for him," Lolita decided. "Why don't we call him 'Perro'?"

"Hi, Perro," Jenna's little sister, Katie, said.

"Woof!" Perro replied. At that, Scott, the collie the PTs were dog-sitting, came running into the room.

Suzie laughed. "Look at their tails! They like each other. Dogs like having friends, too! I'm going to pray that God helps us find Perro's home."

Petie stroked Perro's long, silky ears. "Well, I'm not. I want him to live with me."

After Mrs. Pearson and Perro left, the children practiced their songs for the church Christmas program that night.

That afternoon while the younger children napped, Granny B. gathered the older ones around her. While she read the Bible story of Elizabeth and baby John, the PTs finally had a few minutes alone to talk in another room.

"Sara," Sam began, "you and Jenna are on the Zone 56 planning committee for going back to Whispering Pines tomorrow night, right? Is there anything the rest of us need to know about or bring?"

Maria nodded. "Anything special for snacks? Games?"

Jenna, Le and LaToya smiled at each other. "Sorry, that's top secret."

"Secret?" Sam protested. "We aren't supposed to have secrets from each other!" She felt hurt.

That evening, after Mrs. Pearson came home, she, Sam and Petie took care of Perro. At first Sneezit wagged his tail about it all. Then he got jealous and hid under the couch, whining.

"I know just how you feel, Sneezit," Sam said. "Left out and jealous, right?"

After dinner, Sam helped Petie go over his lines for the program one more time. Then Petie put on his costume. "I feel like a walking bath towel," he griped.

Mrs. Pearson laughed. "You'll do just fine. All you kids will."

They drove by the tree lot to show Petie's costume to Mr. Pearson, who had to work that night as usual. Then it was on to church.

It was a great crowd! Mr. Pearson's boss had donated a beautiful Christmas tree. It had lots of shining ornaments on it, with one glittering star at the very top.

All age groups participated. The Zone 56 members were ushers. The older teens took care of the nursery. Le's mother played the piano. The Senior Sunshiners — a senior citizens group that included LaToya's Granny B. — provided homemade pie.

Sam enjoyed the play that told about the first Christmas night. Then came the Christmas camp choir. But what Sam enjoyed most was joining with everyone to thank God for sending His wonderful Son, Jesus.

Afterward, Aunt Caitlin hugged Sam. "What a great evening!" she exclaimed. "Oh, Sam, I so appreciate what you girls have done this week. So does my sister Candy. In fact, she sent this gift certificate from her pet store for Sneezit and that poor dog that was hit. How is he, by the way?"

Sam looked at the amount on the certificate. One hundred dollars! "He's doing just fine," she said, smiling and hugging her aunt.

"Oh, by the way," Aunt Caitlin added, "I happened to notice a poster about a lost dog on a light pole out in front of the church."

"Oh, one of the PTs must have put it there,"

said Sam. "The camp kids made them to help find Perro's owners."

"No, not your poster," said Aunt Caitlin. "It must have been someone else's. Maybe it's from the person who lost the dog."

Sam rounded up the PTs and they ran outside to read the poster. It had a picture of a golden cocker spaniel on it — one that looked exactly like Perro! The young girl holding him in the picture had a long black ponytail braided with colorful ribbons, and a wonderful smile. She was in a wheelchair. The sign read:

Lost:
Cocker spaniel
Answers to "Cocky."
Grieving family misses him.
Please call Mark Silverhorse at 555-2738.
$500 reward!

"Quick, someone!" Sara said. "Write down that phone number. It looks as though God just answered another prayer!"

· Good News ·
from God's Word

This is the Bible story Granny B. told the children.

Elizabeth's Joy

FROM LUKE 1:5-80

Mary was young when she found out she was going to have baby Jesus. Most of her friends were young, too. But one of her best friends was her relative Elizabeth, an older woman. We don't know if she was Mary's aunt or her cousin, but Mary liked to visit her whenever she could.

Elizabeth and her husband Zechariah were good people. Zechariah was a priest who served God's people in the temple. There was just one thing missing in their lives, something they wanted very much: a baby!

One day an angel appeared to Zechariah with a message: "You are going to have a baby. His name

will be John. He will tell people about Jesus." But Zechariah didn't believe the angel. Instead of believing in God's power, Zechariah thought that he and Elizabeth were too old to be parents. Because he doubted this news, the angel said Zechariah would not be able to talk until the baby was born.

The angel's message did come true. Even though she was old enough to be a grandmother, Elizabeth discovered she was going to be a mother for the very first time. How excited she was! How she praised the Lord!

Meanwhile, an angel came to see Mary, too. He told her that she would have a very special baby, the Son of God. The very same Messiah people had been praying for for years! "You will call His Name Jesus," the angel said.

"But how can I possibly be pregnant?" Mary asked. "I'm not even married yet."

"With God," the angel replied, "nothing is impossible."

Mary was so happy, she jumped up, packed some clothes and hurried off to see her friend Elizabeth. They were thrilled to see each other and share the news of their pregnancies! They knew that God was sending His Son to earth at last.

A Verse to Remember

Nothing is impossible with God.

— *Luke 1:37*

What About You?

Do you really believe that "nothing is impossible with God"? If so, write here what you are praying for God to do. Then pray about it.

_____

_____

_____

_____

God's Blessings Word Search

With God nothing is impossible. This word search contains many of the blessings God has for you. His blessings are not just money or good looks or becoming famous. Instead, look for these good gifts of His love:

air	art	Bible	books
brain	clothes	comfort	time
faith	family	food	friends
fun	games	health	sports
help	home	hope	joy
laughter	life	nature	talents
love	peace	prayer	pets
	room	sleep	

```
N U F A I T H R E Y A R P
S X A R T I T A L E N T S
T X M X X M L I F E H B D
E B I B L E A R O P O R N
P X L J O Y E R O O M A E
L X Y X V X H X D H E I I
E X X R E T H G U A L N R
H B O O K S E R U T A N F
P E E L S P O R T S X X X
X X G A M E S E H T O L C
C O M F O R T P E A C E X
```

The answers are on page 202.

Let's Sing!

This is the special song LaToya taught the Christmas camp choir. After the regular first verse of "Jesus Loves Me," they sang the new second verse. Try it!

In a stable long ago,
Mother Mary whispered low.
Angels sang and shepherds came
To see a baby — what's His name?

Chorus:
His name is Jesus, His name is Jesus,
His name is Jesus,
The Bible tells me so.

Advent Calendar

Cut out or copy and paste the innkeeper onto the Day 10 spot on your Advent calendar. This picture shows the innkeeper in Bethlehem who said there was no room for Mary and Joseph. The Secret Letter for chapter 10 is "R" for "reverent." Write it on line 16.

Chapter 11

Cocky-Doodle-Do

Sam could hardly wait to get home and call the man from the poster, Mr. Silverhorse. "So Cocky does have a home, after all!" she said in the car on the way. "And there's a big reward for him, too!"

But Petie could hardly keep from crying. "He's not Cocky!" he insisted. "He's Perro! And he doesn't look anything like that picture! Perro's our dog!"

When they got home, Mrs. Pearson called the

number on the poster. No one was home, so she left her name and number on the Silverhorses' answering machine. "Now we'll have to wait for them to call us back," she said. "Meanwhile, let's check Perro's bandages and get some dinner ready for your poor dad. He'll be starved when he gets home."

"See!" Petie cried. "You called him 'Perro' too. That's because he's our dog!"

That night after Sam and Petie went to bed, Sam could hear her mother and father talking.

"Were you able to call about that ad during your break today?" Mrs. Pearson asked.

Mr. Pearson sighed. "Yes, but it's not just another job. They want someone to start a SuperService Automotive franchise here in Circleville. I could lease the old Friendly Oil garage since they won't be using it anymore. But that takes money. Money we don't have. So I guess I'll just have to look somewhere else."

"And keep praying," Mrs. Pearson added. "But don't you worry, sweetie, God has something wonderful for you. We just have to find out what it is!"

Sam sighed. Christmas presents were going to be more impossible than ever this year.

The next morning the Christmas camp kids made clay hearts with a little hole at the top. When the hearts were dry, the children painted them. Then they strung yarn through the holes to make necklaces for the residents at Whispering Pines. Afterward, Tony and Le helped them play musical chairs.

Even though it hadn't been that long ago since Zone 56 was at Whispering Pines to decorate, they wanted to go back that night with some presents. The camp kids wanted to help.

Sam and Petie had a lot of fun. But they both were feeling a little sad. Petie didn't want to give up Perro. And Sam felt slighted because no one would tell her what had been planned special for that night's Zone 56 party.

For lunch, Mrs. Jenkins brought over hot alphabet soup with fish-shaped crackers, milk, apples and vanilla pudding. She seemed to be feeling much better. After lunch, Mrs. Thomas called, "Look outside, kids! It's snowing again."

Suddenly her mouth flew open. "Oh, my! Something else is outside, too!" She rushed to the door. "Come in, come in!" she cried.

In walked Mrs. Pearson, a man and the girl in the wheelchair from the "lost" poster — all covered in snowflakes and smiles. Sam's mom introduced them. "Kids, this is Mr. Silverhorse and his daughter, Sonya. They want to thank all of you in person for rescuing and taking care of their lost dog, Cocky."

"We just moved here," Mr. Silverhorse said. "That's why Cocky doesn't have his tags yet. He got out of the yard and I didn't know where to look."

"He's my very best friend," Sonya added. "It's hard enough to transfer to a new school in the middle of the year. And then to lose Cocky, too!"

"Well, welcome to Circleville, Sonya," Sara said. "We older girls all go to Madison Middle School. And to Faith Church. We'd love to introduce you to all our friends."

"In fact," Maria added, "tonight our youth group is going to a nursing home to sing Christmas carols for the patients."

"They're taking presents for the grandmas, too," Lolita said, holding up a heart necklace. "See what we made for them?"

Sonya smiled. "Sounds like fun. I'd love to come along."

"Well, so would I," agreed her father. "Look, we'll get Cocky home and taken care of, then I'll call here to see about rides to the nursing home."

It ended up being a great night! All the Zone 56 members were there, plus some of the younger children and their parents. Miss Kotter also came to see her beloved Ma Jones. She invited Sonya to their Sunday school class. "And you, too, Jenna," she added. Jenna hadn't been to Sunday school yet.

Sonya's dad brought a surprise along: cake and ice cream for everyone! The PTs learned that Sonya's mom had died two years earlier in a car accident, the same accident that had left Sonya in a wheelchair.

After everyone sang Christmas carols, Pastor Andy introduced his own surprise: a ukulele band, made up of Pastor Andy, Jenna, Granny B. and LaToya.

114

So this was Jenna's secret, Sam thought. She felt a tinge of shame for allowing herself to feel hurt over the surprise. Then she relaxed and clapped along with everyone else.

When it was time to go, Jenna told Sonya, "We'd love for you to come over again tomorrow if you're free. You can tell us how Cocky is doing, too."

"I'd love to!" Sonya exclaimed.

As Mr. Silverhorse left, he handed Sam's mother a check and his business card. The reward money! But the card was even more interesting. It read:

Mark Silverhorse
Regional Manager
SuperService Automotive
555-6394

The very company where Sam's dad wanted to work!

· Good News · from God's Word

The PTs had a houseful of people with their Christmas camp. Then there were even more people to entertain at Whispering Pines. But this Bible woman had even more company than that!

Noah's Wife's Full House

FROM GENESIS 5:28-8:22

Did you ever have company at your house? A lot of company? What about dozens and dozens of guests? How would you take care of them all?

That's the situation that faced Noah's wife. At one time, she had just five people in her home — Noah, herself and three little boys. Then her sons grew up and married. So that made three more people in her family.

But one day her family had a new home: a beautiful, large boat. Noah and his sons spent many years building that boat to make it large and strong enough not just for them to survive the flood God would send, but for all their guests. And guess who their guests were? Animals! At least two of every land animal in the world.

That was a lot of guests to care for and feed — like inviting a whole zoo to live at your house! Noah's wife couldn't sit around and be lazy. Her family couldn't fuss and fight with each other. God counted on them to be unselfish workers for Him to save all the animals until the flood was over.

The flood lasted many months, but Noah's family did their job well. Not only was God pleased with them, but so were all their very special guests in this "floating animal hotel."

A Verse to Remember

Be kind and compassionate to one another, forgiving each other.

— **Ephesians 4:32**

What About You?

It's very easy for us to get our own feelings hurt and to hurt other people's feelings, too. What would Jesus have you do in each of these situations? Circle the best answer.

1. You show Emily your pretty, new dress. She goes out and buys one just like it without telling you. Then she wears it before you wear yours! Should you:
   a. Tell her off?
   b. Complain loudly to everyone about it?
   c. Compliment her on her taste then talk about something else?

2. You worked very hard on your science report all by yourself and got a B. Brianna's big brother helped her. She got an A. Should you:
   a. Get angry and start yelling in class?
   b. "Accidentally" spill something on her report?
   c. Ask next time whether you are allowed to have help on your report and then get it?

3. You can't wait until your grandmother visits. But she hugs you, then gives all her attention to your cute little sister. Should you:
   a. Act up so you get some attention, too?
   b. Join your grandmother in playing with your sister so you can all be together?
   c. Shut yourself in your room?

The answers are on page 203.

Let's Eat!

What's your favorite meal? Draw it on the plate 'on the next page. Color in the Christmas designs on the place mat. Then cut out the picture and post it on your refrigerator for your

mom to see. Can she guess what it is? Ask if you can help her cook a real meal like that sometime for your family.

Advent Calendar

Cut out or copy the stable and paste it onto Day 11 on your Advent calendar. This picture shows the stable in Bethlehem where Mary and Joseph stayed. The Secret Letter for chapter 11 is "N" for "not self-centered." Write it on line 17.

Chapter 12

Down-Under Downer

That night after Sam went to bed, she could hear her parents talking. "Oh, Joe!" her mother exclaimed. "This may be the opportunity we've been praying for. Don't you think you ought to talk to this Mark Silverhorse about that SuperService franchise?"

Her father's voice was hesitant. "Well, I don't know, Jean. For a business like that you'd have to put up a lot of money. And you know we don't have it. Since Mr. Silverhorse is in management, he might not understand."

"He might, though. Maybe they have a way for their employees to borrow the money. Let's keep praying about it."

"Well, of course. And we need to figure out what to do with the reward money. As much as we need it ourselves, we should probably pay off Cocky's medical expenses with it, then split up the rest between Sam's friends."

"Oh, I forgot to tell you what I found out about that, Joe. Dr. Grant said Mr. Silverhorse was taking care of Cocky's bill himself. He is a good man, isn't he? Look out there." She pointed out the window. "I think it's snowing again. We're really going to have a white Christmas this year!"

The next morning, Mr. Pearson got up early to shovel the driveway and get the car warmed up for Sam's mom to go to work. Sam and Petie bundled up to go help him. The snow had stopped and the sky was clear and full of stars. To the west, it was still black as night. But in the east, pale fingers of light glimmered over the snow-covered housetops. Smoke drifted out of some chimneys, and Christmas lights sparkled on many of the roofs.

Soon, Mr. Moreno came driving up from his night job as a janitor to face a snow-piled driveway. So they went over to help him, too.

"*Gracias, gracias!*" he exclaimed. "You are too good to me."

"We owe it to you," Sam's dad replied. "Thanks for fixing our car. That was a professional job. Have you worked on cars a lot?"

"*Sí.* Since I was Petie's age, I guess. We were very poor and could only afford older cars. So there was always plenty of work to do on them. Most of our neighbors were in the same boat. My papa and I helped them, too."

"Have you ever had a job as a mechanic?" Petie asked.

"No, *niño*, but I would love to. My janitor job is all right. But motors are what I really love to handle."

Sam's dad reached out his hand. "Sure glad to know that, Pedro. Same with me. If I can find another job working on cars, I'll recommend you to work with me. OK?"

Mr. Moreno gripped his hand. "*Sí.* Now we all better get in out of the cold."

That morning the children at the Christmas camp painted paper doilies to make snowflake pictures. They also played musical chairs, hide-and-seek and make-believe.

At lunch time, Miss Kotter suddenly appeared, wearing a silly old-fashioned hat covered with ribbons and flowers. "Let's play Christmas tea-time!" she announced as she stuck her head in the door. Then she hauled in a box full of goodies.

"I got the afternoon off from work," she explained. "So I told Mrs. Jenkins I'd bring lunch over today and give her a break. I thought we could have an Australian tea time because I've brought a special surprise from Down Under with me: a Christmas present from Bob!"

Thank You, God! Sam prayed. How romantic! Miss Kotter hadn't heard from her sailor boyfriend stationed in the South Pacific for a long time. Sam knew she was very worried about him, so it was good to know he was OK. "What is it, Miss Kotter?"

Miss Kotter laughed. "Now, I told you...it's a surprise. Even to me! I just got the package in the mail before I left the house a few minutes ago. Let's put on the tea kettle and have lunch first. Then I'll open it."

Miss Kotter had made all kinds of tiny sandwiches cut in triangles and fun shapes. There were slices of cucumbers, too, and lots of strange-looking cookies. "People in Australia call cookies 'biscuits,' " Miss Kotter explained. "Or 'bikkies' for short." The adults and older girls got to drink hot tea out of pretty teacups, while the children had hot cocoa.

When they finished, everyone gathered around as Miss Kotter sat down with her Christmas package. It was the size of a shoe box, covered in brown wrapping paper.

But just as she started to open it, someone rang the doorbell. It was Mr. Silverhorse and Sonya. "Thought we'd let you know about Cocky," he said as he helped Sonya wheel in the door. "He's doing just great. The vet says his cast can come off in about three weeks."

Sonya smiled shyly. "If it's all right with everyone, I'd like to stay and help you babysit." Then she smiled. "Since Granny B. has a wheelchair, too, I figured I'd fit in OK."

Sam gave her a hug. "Sonya, you'd fit in even if you were riding a motorcycle!" Then she explained that Miss Kotter was about to open a special package.

"It came all the way from Australia!" Katie added.

Mr. Silverhorse smiled. "Oh, great. I worked in Sydney myself for a while. I'd love to see what you're getting, too, if you don't mind."

Their Sunday school teacher flashed him a smile, then opened her package. First she pulled out  a fluffy toy bear with funny ears and a funnier nose. "A koala bear!" Mr. Silverhorse exclaimed. "I saw a lot of real ones in Australia. Kangaroos, too."

Miss Kotter hugged the cuddly toy. "I'll call him 'Aus,' " she decided.

"You mean, like the 'Wizard of Aus'?" teased Jenna. Everyone laughed.

Then Miss Kotter pulled out two letters. "This one's from Bob," she announced. "I don't recognize the name on the other one." She started reading aloud:

Dear Kitty,

You will always be dear to me. This is the hardest letter I have written in my entire life. I won't be coming home soon. In fact, I won't be coming home at all!

Their teacher gasped and turned pale. Mrs. Thomas grabbed her so she wouldn't fall over. *Oh, no!* Sam cried to herself. This package was supposed to be an answer to prayer. What in the world had gone wrong? Didn't God still answer prayer?

· Good News · from God's Word

How hurt and disappointed Miss Kotter was! Here is someone else who became very disappointed about what she was hoping for.

Sarah's Hope

FROM GENESIS 11:28-18:15

Sarah loved babies. She loved to play with her friends' babies and she loved playing with little Lot, her nephew. When his parents died, she and her husband, Abraham, had adopted him. But more than anything else she wanted a baby of her own. She prayed and prayed about it. God promised her she would have a child someday.

Ten years passed. Then 20. Then 30. And still, there was no baby! Sarah turned 70, 80, 85…still no baby! By now she was very old, old enough to be a grandmother. But she couldn't be a grandmother if she had never been a mother! *Maybe God was mistaken*, she thought. Maybe she should just quit praying about it. Maybe she should stop hoping and believing God's promises.

But one day when she was 89, God's angel told Abraham, "Next year you'll be a father, and Sarah will be a mother." Sarah laughed at that. It was such a lovely thought. But she was too old now, far too old.

Guess what? The next year, when she was 90, she did become a mother. The angel instructed Abraham and Sarah to name the baby "Isaac," which meant "laughing" in their language. Sarah laughed with the joy that God had kept His promises even though she didn't believe Him at first.

A Verse to Remember

Praise awaits you, O God...
O you who hear prayer.

— Psalm 65:1-2

What About You?

Have you ever had a real disappointment — something you had really hoped would happen but it didn't? Write about it here.

_____

_____

_____

Maybe you still feel badly about it. If so, why don't you ask God right now to help you feel better? He can, you know. In fact, His Holy Spirit is called the "Comforter," just because He helps people feel better and have hope and joy again.

Tea for Two

You can have a tea party like Miss Kotter gave for the PTs and the Christmas camp kids. You could invite your mother, grandmother, aunt, a favorite teacher or a friend. Or even several of them!

You can use one type of tea or a variety. You may use tea leaves, but tea bags are easier. You'll also need boiling water in a pan or tea kettle, cups and saucers for all your guests, sugar (sugar cubes are fun!), sugar substitute and milk or cream. Just be careful about handling the hot water, the hot pot and the china cups and saucers. Make dainty sweets or sandwiches (see below). And, of course, you will need a teapot.

Set up everything as attractively as possible — tablecloth, flowers (real or artificial) and pretty dishes. Wear party clothes. For even more fun, use a toy tea set.

You'll find everything suits you to a "tea"!

Grandwiches

Here is how to make some special, fun sandwiches — Grandwiches — for your tea party:

1. Get a loaf of white or wheat sandwich bread, or one of each.
2. Lay out the slices on a cutting board.
3. Lightly spread half of the slices with mayonnaise or a mayonnaise substitute.
4. Spread the other slices with ham salad, tuna salad (see recipe on page 130) or chicken salad. For a taste sensation, top some with olive slices, cucumber slivers or sliced cherry tomatoes.
5. Place each mayonnaise slice with a salad slice. It's fun to combine wheat and white in the same sandwich!
6. Slice off the crusts.
7. Cut each sandwich diagonally into fourths. You could also use cookie cutters to cut the sandwiches into shapes. Another idea: stack three slices together before cutting to make club-style sandwiches.

continued on next page...

8. Attractively arrange your Grandwiches on a plate. Add pickles or deviled eggs to the plate for extra color and more yumminess.

Tuna Salad

What You Need

- 6-oz. can tuna
- 1 tablespoon mayonnaise or mayonnaise substitute
- 1 tablespoon relish
- 1 tablespoon finely-chopped celery

What to Do

1. Drain the tuna in the sink.
2. Mix all of the ingredients together in a bowl.
3. Spread on bread or crackers, or scoop onto a plate of lettuce. This recipe will make three generous sandwiches.

Your Cup of Tea

On the next page is a simple outline of a cup and saucer. Decorate it the way you'd like your own cup to look. You can also copy this picture to use as invitations for your tea party.

Advent Calendar

Cut out or copy and glue the star onto the Day 12 spot of your Advent calendar. This is the special star that shone over the stable where Mary and Joseph stayed. The Secret Letter for chapter 12 is "H" for "hopeful." Write it on line 7.

Chapter 13

When It Rains, It Snows!

With her arm around Miss Kotter, Mrs. Thomas said firmly, "Honey, I think you'd better read the rest in private." Then she led her — still clutching the two letters — upstairs to a bedroom.

Everyone looked around awkwardly. Lolita

started to cry.

Mr. Silverhorse picked up the toy koala bear and pretended it was a puppet. "Hi there!" he said in a high, squeaky voice. "I'm 'Aus.' I come from Down Under. Do you know what 'down under' means?"

Mrs. Thomas brought out a globe. Sonya's dad held the bear against the globe and had it "stand" on Australia. "Help!" he squeaked. "I'm falling!"

The children started to giggle. Soon he had them laughing along with him. They pretended to climb trees like koalas do, and jump around the room like kangaroos. He taught them to say "cheerio" and "ta-da," which both mean "good-bye." Meanwhile, Granny B. and the PTs gathered up Miss Kotter's other belongings and helped her leave by the back door.

Finally, the younger children settled down with Granny B. for story time. Sonya stayed to help, parking her wheelchair right next to Granny B.'s. The PTs and Mr. Silverhorse followed Mrs. Thomas to another room, where LaToya's mom explained what had happened.

"The bottom line," she sighed, "is that while Bob's been in the Navy he has met someone else. A woman named Cindy Sontag. They're both Christians, and they both feel called to work as missionaries in Australia. That other letter was from her. Both Bob and Cindy seem very sincere, and are trying hard to show Kitty how sorry they are to hurt her. But of course she's very hurt anyway."

"The poor lady!" Mr. Silverhorse exclaimed. "What can we do to help?"

"She'll need to keep busy," Sam decided. "She was already planning to work at the rescue mission as much as possible this Christmas. Maybe we can go, too, and support her — when we're not babysitting, of course."

Mr. Silverhorse nodded. "You'll have to tell me more about this rescue mission. Since my regular work won't start 'til next week, I have time to volunteer." Then standing up he added, "Well, I'd better go. Please tell Sonya I'll be back to get her later."

Sam glanced at the clock. "We'd better go give Granny B. a break," she said. But inside all she could think about was poor Miss Kotter. How awful she must feel! *Please comfort her, dear God*, she prayed.

The children bundled up and ran outside to play in the snow. Then they came back inside, unbundled and had cocoa and cookies.

Then the phone rang. It was Jenna's father.

When Jenna hung up, she was as pale as Miss Kotter had been. "They've had to rush Mom to the hospital," she said. "Dad said for me to stay here with Katie. But I want to be with Mom!" And she started to cry. Katie started crying, too.

Maria hugged them both. "My papa could drive you there," she said. "But you'd have to stay out in the waiting room by yourself, which wouldn't be any fun. So why don't you both come over to my house with me and Lolita and the boys? We can have dinner there. You can stay overnight with us, too, if your dad says it's OK. Like a big slumber party!"

Mrs. Moreno welcomed Jenna and Katie with open arms. "You are going to love the twin babies!" she said. "Our twins have been so much fun!"

Later that evening Mr. Jenkins called from the hospital. "Hi, Jenna! Hi, Katie!" he said. "The babies haven't come yet, but your mother is doing all right. And guess who's with me in the waiting room? Kitty Kotter, Pedro Moreno, Jim Thomas, Mark Silverhorse, Pastor McConahan from Jenna's church and LaToya's big sister, Tina! Can you believe it?

"And Joe Pearson called to say he'd come over as soon as he got out of work tonight. I can't believe how helpful everyone's been! They don't even really know me!"

After work that night, Mr. Pearson was exhausted. It was almost Christmas now and the crowds at the tree lot had him working twice as hard. But instead of resting, he ate a quick dinner and rushed on over to the hospital to be with Mr. Jenkins, too. He knew that it was important for all of them to show God's love to the Jenkins family, who were not Christians.

Later, he called home with some wonderful news. The twins had been born. Two adorable little girls! They were premature so they were very small. But they were in perfect health. Mrs. Jenkins was fine, too. And, yes, these Christmas babies had Christmas names: Noel and Holly!

He also said that all of the friends in the

waiting room had a wonderful time talking and praying together. He and Maria's dad even had a chance to talk to Mr. Silverhorse about their dream of running their own auto service shop. Tina was a real comfort to Miss Kotter, too. In fact, Miss Kotter was so impressed with Tina's compassionate spirit that she invited her to work with her at the rescue mission the next day.

As Sam brushed her teeth and pulled on her pajamas, her head was spinning. So much good news! *Now, dear God,* Sam prayed, *if Dad can just find a job. And then maybe all of us could get Christmas presents. At least one a piece! But if not, well, that's OK, too. I still love You anyway!*

· Good News · from God's Word

The Faith Church families were glad to help the Jenkins family when they needed it. In this Bible story, who is able to help Hagar in her time of need?

Hagar's New Friends

FROM GENESIS 21:14-19

Hagar grew up in Egypt. That's where all her family lived, and where she met Sarah and Abraham.

They were very rich, important people. When they asked her to be their servant, she was glad to go with them. They worshipped the one true God. She wanted to worship Him, too.

But Sarah and Abraham didn't stay in Egypt. They moved on to Israel. Now Hagar became homesick. Later, she had a little boy named Ishmael. As the boy grew older, Sarah and Hagar began to fight and fuss. The disagreements became especially bad after Sarah also had a little boy. Abraham's happy home wasn't happy any more.

God told Abraham he should send Hagar back home to her family in Egypt. This wasn't a very long trip, but she lost her way anyway. Soon she and Ishmael were out in the desert with no food or water. How frightened they were! Poor Hagar sat down on a rock and began to sob.

But even though she didn't know where she was, God did. "Hagar, what's the matter?" God asked. "Don't be afraid." Then God showed her where to find a well of water. Other people who lived near the well helped her, too. In fact, she decided to stay with these new friends and live with them. She was so glad that God didn't just care for rich people like Abraham, but also for poor servants, like her and Ishmael.

A Verse to Remember

Carry each other's burdens.

— **Galatians 6:2**

Advent Calendar

Cut out or copy this shepherd and paste it onto Day 13 on your Advent calendar. This picture shows a shepherd with his sheep on that first Christmas night. The Secret Letter for chapter 13 is "S" for "sensitive to others." Write it on the line for Day 5.

Kitchy-Kitchy-Koo!

What would you name twins? Write names below the twins on the next page. Then design their clothes as you might dress them.

Alexandria   Cornelia

Where Will It All End?

The last letter of each of the 22 names in the chain below is the first letter of another name. This chain is like people who share God's love with others. When one hears the Good News, he or she can tell another and that person can tell another.

See how many names you can find (don't forget: the chain keeps going even at the ends of the first two lines!). The answers are on page 203.

BETTYVONNEDWARDANIELINDADRIA
EDONNANNESTHEROSARTOMITCHEAT
ERICKURTYLEROBRIANANGELANDY

_____   _____

_____   _____

_____   _____

_____   _____

_____   _____

_____   _____

_____   _____

_____   _____

_____   _____

Chapter 14

Arms Full of Love

The next day, Suzie came to Christmas camp clutching an armful of stuffed bears. "She insisted on bringing them in for the new babies," Aunt Caitlin explained, laughing. "She wants to give them all her other old toys, too."

"Me, too!" cried Juan, holding up an old wooden train. "For the babies!"

"What can I give?" asked Lolita.

Mrs. Thomas laughed. "Kids, those babies are

too young to play with your toys. But I know who is old enough to enjoy them. The children down at the rescue mission! Would you like Tina and Miss Kotter to take them there for you?"

The children were excited at that idea, so all their parents were contacted to see if they had any other old, clean toys, blankets or clothes to bring the next day for the shelter, too. When Miss Kotter mentioned this need for gifts to her friend Ma Jones at Whispering Pines, Ma spread the word. The residents took up a collection, and Miss Kotter used the money to buy new toys and other presents for the rescue mission.

Back at the camp, Granny B. told the children the Bible story about baby Jesus. The kids decided to draw pictures of baby Jesus for Jenna and Katie's twin sisters. " 'Cause they're Christmas babies, too!" one of the kids said.

While the children colored, the PTs held a business meeting to discuss a Christmas present for Miss Kotter.

"She's been through so much unhappiness," sighed Jenna. "I just wish we could give her a whole year of happiness instead!"

"We could," decided LaToya, "if we give her a calendar. A very special calendar. One we make up ourselves."

Le clapped her hands. "Yes! Mom's computer

has special software for making calendars. We can add pictures to it, too. What if everyone gives me a snapshot you've taken sometime over the year? We'll scan them into the computer and have a different picture for every month."

"Great!" cried Sara. "We could even add jokes and favorite Bible verses."

Sonya smiled shyly. "A year with you PTs would have to be a happy one," she said. "It must be wonderful to be in your club."

Sam gave her a hug. "What do you mean, Sonya? You're already in it!"

Sonya looked puzzled. "What do you mean? I don't even know how to join!"

Sam laughed. "Sonya, a PT is just a girl our age who loves God and wants to serve Him."

"That's it?" Sonya asked.

Maria giggled. "No, four more things. She should live in Circleville. She should go to our school and our church. And she should wear a ponytail."

Now it was Sonya's turn to giggle. "Well, then, I guess I did join the club, didn't I?"

Soon Mr. Jenkins stopped by for Jenna and Katie. "Let's go see your new sisters, girls," he said. "Then we need to get the house straightened up. Your mom and sisters get to come home tomorrow!"

Just then Granny B. wheeled in with Mrs. Thomas right behind her. "This casserole and cake will be good for dinner tomorrow," LaToya's mom said. "Then Karen won't have to worry about meals for a few days while she gets used to those two new babies."

"And here are some blankets I made for the twins," Granny B. added. She held up two white baby blankets. Both of them had holly leaves and berries appliqued on them.

Jenna and Katie gave her a big hug. "Oh, Granny B.! They're just beautiful!" Jenna said. "You'll have to come over and see the babies soon yourself! Promise?"

By the time Sam and Petie got back to their own house that afternoon, they were both so worn out that they just plopped down in front of the TV. When their mother came in from work, she was tired, too. "Let's just have beans-and-franks tonight," Mom suggested. "With hot biscuits and jelly."

"Sounds great," Sam agreed. "I'll put the biscuits in the oven." She loved to open canned biscuits and hear the "pop" sound from the can — like a firecracker.

Petie jumped up. "And I'll set the table."

Sam stared at him. "You? Are you sick? I don't think you've ever set the table in your life!"

He grinned. "Maybe I was never this hungry before!"

Just then the phone rang. It was Grandma and Grandpa Pearson. They'd be there tomorrow!

Her dad had good news that night, too. His boss gave all the workers a $100 bonus for Christmas!

Maybe we will have a great Christmas, after all, Sam thought. Fancy presents, or not!

· Good News ·
from God's Word

This is the Bible story Granny B. told the children.

Mary's Christmas Present

FROM LUKE 2:1-20

Mary and Joseph were happy in their new
marriage. They loved each other and they loved God.
For many years God had promised to send His Son to
the world. Now it was time for that Son to be born.
And Mary would be His mother! Mary and Joseph
looked forward to sharing their little home in
Nazareth with their new baby boy.

Then one day they received sad news. The
Emperor, Caesar Augustus, passed a new law. It said

that everyone had to pay a special tax in their hometowns. Because Joseph's family came from Bethlehem, that's where he and Mary had to go.

The journey on the donkey was difficult for Mary because she was due to have her baby soon. Even worse, when they finally reached Bethlehem, hot and tired, they found that all of the rooms for rent in the crowded city were filled. They only had one place to go: a dirty, smelly stable with the animals.

And of all the nights to give birth to God's Son, it was in this stable that Mary had baby Jesus. It was the first Christmas!

What a night! The angels sang! The shepherds came and worshipped Him while Mary rocked baby Jesus to sleep in her arms. He was the very best Christmas present of all!

A Verse to Remember

A Savior has been born to you;
he is Christ the Lord.

— *Luke 2:11*

What About You?

What was your favorite Christmas present?

_____

_____

What's the best gift you ever gave?

_____

_____

What does Christmas mean to you, besides gifts?

_____

_____

It's a Bear World, After All!

Suzie wanted to share her old teddy bears with other children. On page 151 is a bear you can share. You can color the picture, or use it as a pattern for a stuffed toy, washcloth or hand puppet.

Stuffed Toy

What You Need

• fabric

• scissors

• needle

• thread

• markers

• stuffing

What to Do

1. Fold the fabric in half and trace the pattern on it.

continued on next page…

Felt, flannel or fake fur work especially well for this craft.

2. Cut the pattern from the two thicknesses.

3. Before you stitch the two sides together, draw features on the bear with markers. Other ideas: stitch them, cut them from felt scraps and glue them on or sew on buttons.

4. After you finish the features, stitch together the two sides of the body all around the outside edges, leaving the top open.

5. Stuff the bear with pieces of cotton, old cloth, polyester stuffing or nylon netting. You can leave the ears unstuffed or slide in cardboard circles.

6. Sew the top closed.

Washcloth

What You Need

- old towel or washcloth
- scissors
- needle
- thread
- netting

What to Do

1. Fold the towel in half.

2. Trace the pattern on the washcloth and cut it out.

3. Turn the cloth inside out and sew the edges

together, leaving an open space for stuffing.

4. Turn the cloth back the right way, and stuff with netting. Sew closed.

Hand Puppet

What You Need

- fabric
- scissors
- needle
- thread

What to Do

1. Fold the fabric and trace the pattern on it so the head is at the fold.

2. Cut out the bear. Be careful to not cut the fold!

3. Cut a slit on the back side as indicated in the pattern.

4. Draw, glue or stitch a face on the bear.

5. Turn the bear inside out with the face on the inside.

6. Sew a seam all the way around the edge of the puppet. Leave space for your hand at the bottom edge.

7. Turn the puppet right side out. Stuff enough netting in the head to keep it from flopping over, but leave room in the neck to insert your middle finger when you use the puppet.

continued on next page…

8. Stuff the four paws, leaving room in the top two paws for your index and ring fingers.

9. Lightly stuff the "tummy," leaving room to insert your hand through the slot and keep it inside.

10. To work the puppet, use your middle finger to help it nod or shake its head, and your other two fingers to work its arms. You may press your thumb over your little finger inside the puppet to keep those fingers still.

11. Name your bear. Use your bear to "tell a story" to a young friend!

Advent Calendar

Cut out or copy the angel and paste it on Day 14 on your Advent calendar. This picture shows an angel that first Christmas night telling the shepherds the Good News about baby Jesus' birth. The Secret Letter for chapter 14 is "R" for "reaching out to others." Write it on line 8.

Chapter 15

Me Clean?
That's Mean!

The next morning, Sam awoke to a strange sound. Bang, bang! Swish, swish! Push, push! Zoom, zoom! She walked into the kitchen, rubbing her eyes. "What in the world," she stuttered. "It's not even 6 yet, Mom! It's still practically the middle of the night!"

Mrs. Pearson whizzed around the kitchen like a tornado with an apron on. "Yes, but there's so much to do and so little time to do it! I'm glad you're up. You two kids need to clean your rooms before your grandparents come, plus dust the living room and vacuum. I'm going in early to work so I can take the afternoon off. I've got to go grocery shopping, and take a pot of soup over to the Jenkinses. That poor woman will have her hands full with those babies. Then I'll drive in to Danville to pick up your grandparents at the airport. And somewhere in all this we still have Christmas shopping to do! Maybe tomorrow."

Suddenly her mother sat down. "Whew! I'm already tired. Better have another cup of coffee."

Sam pulled her robe tighter in the morning chill. "But I have to work, too, today, Mom, at the Christmas camp. Remember?"

"Yes, but you'll have some time before you leave and after you come home. How about some oatmeal for breakfast? That'll give you some energy to get going!"

As her mother started scrubbing the kitchen counters, Sam fixed herself some instant oatmeal. Inside, she was steaming as much as her cereal. Work, work, work! She'd spent her whole vacation working. Was there no end to it? When did Christmas start being fun?

Petie wasn't any happier about the whole thing. "Clean my room?" he protested. "What about morning cartoons? Can't I just shove everything into my closet? Grandma won't look in there!"

By the time they left for LaToya's house, Sam and Petie were irritable and exhausted. But it was the last day of Christmas camp. They couldn't disappoint the other kids now by not showing up.

Soon those other children began arriving, too, along with bags and boxes full of dolls, balls, blocks, games, toys and bags of clean, ironed clothes. "They're all for the rescue mission," Katie explained. "Do you think the kids will be glad?"

"Oh, yes," Sam replied. "And so will Jesus, because you have been so kind."

After a while Miss Kotter came with Mr. Silverhorse and Sonya. Miss Kotter was thrilled with all the donations. Mr. Silverhorse and LaToya's big sister, Tina, loaded them all into Mr. Silverhorse's van, then they left for the mission with Miss Kotter.

But then things started going wrong. Sam's dad called and asked if Sara's big brother, Tony, wanted to make some extra cash by coming down to the Christmas tree lot to help out. He left immediately.

"No fair!" Sara protested. "He was supposed to help us with our games."

"No problem," Sonya replied. "Granny B. and I can play wheelchair hockey with them. Can't we, Granny B.?"

Granny B. smiled and nodded.

Petie ran home to get his plastic ice hockey sticks. Sonya cut some plastic picnic plates in half for "pucks." The older kids bundled up and ran out to the back patio. After they helped Mr. Thomas clear the snow off the patio bricks, he showed them how to play "ice hockey" using the two wheelchairs as goals. Everyone was soon rolling in the snow with laughter.

Then Maria remembered lunch. With Mrs. Jenkins in the hospital, they had been winging it with peanut butter sandwiches, apples and milk. But now they were out of peanut butter and apples. What would they eat?

Just then her mother, like an angel in disguise, arrived with a tray of hot tacos and grapes. She quickly  heated up a pot of tomato soup.

At Bible story time, Granny B. had a headache. "Oh, what will we do now?" Le worried. Then she had an idea. She asked LaToya's mom for some old towels and sheets so the children could make costumes. Then they acted out the Bible story of the first Christmas night!

"That was fun!" Suzie cried. "I wish Christmas camp would never end." She gave Sam a big hug.

At the end of the day, the PTs added up their camp money. After taking out expenses and an offering, they each got $50. It sure didn't seem like much for a whole week's work! But Sam knew that it would really help her family to have a brighter Christmas. So would the reward money for finding and taking care of Cocky, which the girls and their families had also agreed to divide evenly.

Back at the Pearsons, when Sam and Petie walked in the door, they found a note:

I went to the airport.
Please feed Sneezit.
Put your coats and everything away.
And don't mess up anything!
Love,
Mom

"More work!" Sam grumbled. After they put everything away, they turned on the Christmas tree lights. How beautifully they twinkled! Each year, the floor beneath the tree would be piled high with presents. But this time the floor was empty. Then they turned on the TV.

"Look, Sam!" Petie cried. "A Christmas parade!"

"This is a *posada*," the newscaster announced. "In Mexican culture, people dress up like Mary and Joseph and go through the streets looking for a place to stay. Others put little lanterns out in their front yards to help show Mary and Joseph the way."

"That's like our church program!" Petie said. "Like the first Christmas night!"

As Sam watched, all of the resentment in her heart about gifts and work melted away. This was what was important, she realized, God sending His Son, Jesus, into the world to show His love.

Just then the door flew open. In rushed Grandma and Grandpa Pearson. Sam and Petie hugged them both. Yes, this was what Christmas was about: love and more love. Sam was so happy, she even hugged Sneezit!

· Good News ·
from God's Word

Don't you sometimes wish you could have seen baby Jesus for yourself? So did Anna. And then something wonderful happened. Read on.

Anna's Labor of Love

FROM LUKE 2:21-38

When Anna was a young woman, she loved God very much and believed His Word. So did her young husband. They longed for the day God would send His Son to earth.

Then one day her husband died. She was so sad! She didn't have any children, so she was all alone. Then Anna thought, *Since I don't have a family*

to take care of, I'll take care of God's House. So she stayed in the temple in Jerusalem day and night, praying and worshipping. She asked God to send His Son.

Many years passed. Now Anna was an old woman of 84. But she still spent all her time in God's House. That's why she was there the day something wonderful happened. Mary and Joseph brought in baby Jesus!

"Oh, thank You, God!" she cried. Then she started telling everyone that this little boy was the Savior they had been praying for all these years. All the people there started praising God. Anna praised Him most of all.

A Verse to Remember

You are to give him the name Jesus,
because he will save his people from their sins.

— *Matthew 1:21*

What About You?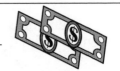

What are your daily chores?

_____

Your weekly chores?

_____

Do you get an allowance? _____

Do you have to do chores to get your allowance? _____

How much is your allowance? _____

On what do you usually spend it?

_____

Do you feel you have too many chores or too few?

_____

Who can help you do your chores with a smile?

_____

Everything But the Kitchen Sink

Here's a fun quiz about common kitchen objects and chores. Write one of the words from the list on page 160 in the sentences that follow. For the answers, see page 203.

1. This whole house has gone to _sweeping_!

2. Let's make some _pot_ changes.

3. She's been _scrubbed_ from the team.

4. Ashes to ashes, dust to _dust_.

5. You could cut the fog with a _knife_.

continued on next page…

6. All right, _clean_ up your act!

7. I saw what you took. _Fork_ it over!

8. It's hot enough to _fry_ an egg on the sidewalk.

9. That does it! You're _toast_!

10. Don't go off half-_baked_.

A. dust — B. fry C. clean

D. pot — E. baked F. scrubbed

G. knife —H. toast I. sweeping

J. fork

Advent Calendar

Cut out or copy and paste Mary and Joseph onto Day 15 on your Advent calendar. This picture shows Mary and Joseph that first Christmas night. The Secret Letter for chapter 15 is "U" for "understanding." Write it on line 4.

Chapter 16

The Day Before Christmas

Sam and Petie helped their grandparents bring in their suitcases. But instead of being full of clothes, the bags were full of presents! What fun to pile them up under the Christmas tree! Just like old times.

"Sam, please take Grandma and Grandpa up to their room," Mrs. Pearson said. "I'll get dinner on the table."

They all sat down to eat meat loaf, mashed potatoes, stewed apples and baked beans. But first, they held hands while Grandpa led in prayer. Then they started right in.

Just then the doorbell rang. It was Aunt Caitlin, Uncle Todd and Suzie! After there were hugs all around, Mrs. Pearson set more places at the table and Todd's family sat down, too.

Soon Grandma and Grandpa began telling stories about Christmases when they were young, and when Sam's dad and Uncle Todd were young. Petie seemed to enjoy the stories about his dad most of all. "Oh, cool!" he crowed. "Now I have something to tease Dad about!"

When Suzie's family left, Grandpa Pearson and Petie bundled up and went down to see Mr. Pearson at the tree lot. The women cleaned up the kitchen and put things away. Sam noticed that when she helped her mother and grandmother like that, it didn't seem like work at all. It was fun!

When Grandpa Pearson and Petie returned, Mr. Pearson was with them. Mrs. Pearson heated up his dinner and everyone talked some more. Finally, it was bedtime. Because Sam's grandparents would be sleeping in her room, she pulled some sheets and blankets out of the linen closet to make herself a bed on the living room couch.

Sam turned on the Christmas tree lights and some quiet Christmas music. Then she started writing a to-do list. Tomorrow was Christmas Eve and she hadn't even started her shopping yet! She'd really have to rush around to get everything done at the stores up the street and the mall, too. And everything would be so crowded!

Soon Sneezit pitter-pattered down the stairs and crawled up on the couch beside her. Petie was not far behind.

He held out two $10 bills. "Grandma said one is for you and one is for me," he explained in a whisper. "I want to buy Christmas presents with mine. But I don't know how. I can't even figure out what things cost. Could you help me?"

"No!" she wanted to shout. "There's not time!" Instead, she hugged her little brother. "Sure, kid. Now say your prayers and get to bed."

The next morning Sam was still brushing her teeth when the doorbell rang. It was Aunt Caitlin and Suzie. "I'm really in a bind," her aunt said. "Yesterday was supposed to be my last day at the pet shop. But my sister Candy is sick today. If you don't mind letting Suzie stay here 'til I get off, I'd really appreciate it! Here's some money for her lunch."

"Now don't you worry about a thing," Mrs. Pearson replied. "We love having her."

But Sam looked sad. *Mom was going to take me Christmas shopping today,* she whimpered to herself. *Now what will I do?*

Petie was also disappointed.

Sam thought and prayed about it. "Don't worry," she said to Petie with a smile. "I have a plan. We're going to organize a Christmas caravan!"

Soon afterward, a whole troop of laughing,

singing PTs headed up to the local stores. They were joined by half a dozen younger children, who took turns pulling Granny B.'s old grocery cart.

The older girls helped each of the younger ones with their purchases, then made their own, too. The shopping got very confusing, especially with all the crowds. But as soon as anything was paid for, it was put in a separate bag for each shopper, and then in the shopping cart. Sonya kept the cart by her wheelchair to guard it while the others shopped. When they were all done, Maria covered the cart with a big, thick towel so nothing would fall out. Then Sam treated everyone to hamburgers for lunch with the money Aunt Caitlin had left.

Back at Sam's house, Grandma Pearson helped everyone wrap their presents. She even showed the older girls how to make fancy bows.

It was a fun, hectic time to be surrounded by piles of brightly colored paper. Sneezit kept yipping and tumbling and getting himself tangled up in the ribbons. Then he yapped some more.

"Do you have any special plans for Christmas this year, Le?" Sara asked.

Le nodded. "You know the music director at the Vietnamese church? Well, he and Mom have been dating, mostly going to church concerts. Anyway, we're all getting together for Christmas dinner. He has two little boys. Their mother's been dead a long time, just like my dad."

"Are you happy about your mother dating again, Le?" Jenna asked.

"I think so. Of course, I'm kind of scared about our lives changing so quickly. But I'm awfully glad about her being happy again. You know, Mom was so sad. Then she became a Christian and I think that has helped her to be much happier. Now she loves Christian songs and Bible stories and church services. Plus God brought someone new into her life. It's amazing what can happen when you follow Him!"

Sam gave her a hug. "What about you, Sonya? Do you think your dad will start dating again?"

Sonya was quiet a minute. "I guess I never thought about it. But I would love to have a mom again." Suddenly she grinned. "And I just thought of someone who would be a perfect mom! But I'm not going to tell who it is!"

Just then Mr. Silverhorse and Miss Kotter came by. "Jenna, are you and Katie ready?" Miss Kotter asked. "Your mother asked us to drop you at home. She said you can invite some of the other girls to see the babies, too, if you want."

Only Sonya and Sam were able to go. How cute those babies were! They couldn't have looked more alike if they had been mirrors! "How do you tell them apart?" Sam asked.

Mrs. Jenkins laughed. "I'm keeping their little ID bracelets on them for a while. But do you know something? They might look alike, but I know God made each one special and different. Isn't that wonderful?"

Jenna brushed her little sisters' hair into tiny topknots. "Look, Sam!" she laughed. "They'll have enough hair soon to be Ponytail Girls, too!"

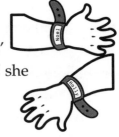

· Good News · from God's Word

Both Sam and LaToya have loving grandmothers. So did someone in the following Bible story.

Lois' Grandmotherly Love

FROM 2 TIMOTHY 1:1-5; 2:1, 5; 3:14-17

Grandchildren love their grandparents. And grandparents love their grandchildren. Grandparents are so proud of their grandchildren!

That's the way Lois felt about her little grandson, Timothy. Timothy also loved his grandmother Lois, who was a Christian. Timothy's mother, Eunice, was also a Christian.

Even though both women were busy, they taught him God's Word, even when he was just a little boy. They helped him read and memorize Bible verses. They told him about God's Son, Jesus, whom they both loved very much.

By the time Timothy was a teenager, he had made his own decision for Christ. Soon after that, God called him to be a missionary helper and a pastor. That's why we have two books in the New Testament with his name on them. They are letters written to him by Paul.

How glad Timothy was for the loving help of both his mother and grandmother that made him ready to serve God!

A Verse to Remember

Keep...sound teaching, with faith and love in Christ Jesus.

— 2 Timothy 1:13

Remember how memorizing God's Word helped Timothy? Try to memorize the verses in this book. They will help you, too!

What About You?

Do you know your grandmothers' names? If so, write them here. Then write something you love about each of them.

Grandmother: _____

What I love about her: _____

_____

_____

Grandmother: _____

What I love about her: _____

_____

_____

Now, write letters to or call your grandmothers and let them know how much you love them!

Your Family Tree

In the top row of the family tree on the next page, write your father's parents' names and then your mother's parents' names. On the second row, write your father's and mother's names. On the third row, write your name. You may also draw each person's picture or cut and glue pictures of the people on your tree (ask permission first). If you have brothers or sisters, write in their names at the bottom.

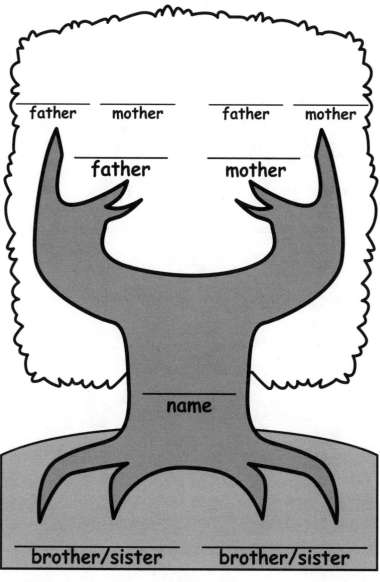

father   mother   father   mother

father   mother

name

brother/sister   brother/sister

Advent Calendar

Cut out or copy baby Jesus and paste
Him onto Day 16 on your Advent calendar.
This picture shows baby Jesus in the stable that
first Christmas night. The Secret Letter for chapter 16
is "O" for "on God's side." Write it on line 15.

Chapter 17

The Night Before Christmas

By the time the Silverhorses and Miss Kotter brought Sam back from visiting the new twins, it was time for dinner. Grandma Pearson had prepared a big pot of beef stew and a hot pan of cornbread.

"Come on and join us!" she called out to the visitors. "I've made enough for an army. That way you won't have to cook tonight. And…there's coconut pie for later!"

There wasn't room for everyone to sit together at the dining room table, so Mrs. Pearson set up a card table in the living room. Miss Kotter joined the three kids there. Sonya especially enjoyed hearing Miss Kotter tell about growing up in an orphanage and how Ma Jones from the orphanage was still her good friend today.

"Let's call her up!" Sonya said. So they dialed Ma Jones over at Whispering Pines. Then everyone yelled, "Merry Christmas!" to her over the phone. Just then the front door flew open. "Merry Christmas yourself!" Sam's dad exclaimed.

Sam ran to hug him and take off his work jacket. "You're home early!" she cried.

He grinned. "There's not a single tree left on the lot. Not even a branch! So we closed up."

"I just finished eating," Sam's mom said. "You can have my seat at the table after you wash up."

A little later, the whole gang from Sam's house walked into Faith Church. Sam waved to Sara and Tony. And to Le and her mother. They were sitting next to her mother's new boyfriend and his little boys. She could even see Maria's family and LaToya's. But not Jenna's. Her family would all be home together tonight with their new babies. Last of all, Sam saw Suzie's family. Aunt Caitlin and Uncle Todd hurried over to sit with Grandma and Grandpa Pearson.

It was wonderful to sing Christmas carols!

LaToya and some other Zone 56 members played along on guitars. In between the songs, Pastor McConahan read about the first Christmas from the Bible.

"We've all been celebrating Christmas since we were children," he said. "But sometimes we get so caught up in presents and decorations and parties that we forget what it's all about. I want you to think: What does Christmas really mean to you?"

The pastor didn't really want an answer; he wanted people to think about it. But just like that, up shot someone's arm. Little Suzie's!

She jumped right up. "It means God loves us," she said. "That's why He sent dear baby Jesus. He even loves naughty little girls like me. Thank You, God. I love You, too!" And she sat back down.

Aunt Caitlin started to get tears in her eyes, Sam noticed. So did Grandma Pearson. And so did Uncle Todd. And so did Pastor McConahan! He blew his nose. " 'And a little child shall lead them,' " he

quoted from the Bible. Then everyone sang "Jesus Loves Me." Of course, it wasn't a Christmas carol, but no one minded one bit.

At the end of the service everyone held lit candles and sang "Silent Night." By now Sonya's eyes were tearing up, too. "It's all so beautiful! I hate to go home!"

"Stay at my house tonight. It would be fun!" Le suggested.

"Then come on over to our house tomorrow," Sam added. "And bring Cocky with you to play with Sneezit."

"Your papa can come for coffee at our house," added Mr. Moreno. "I'd like to show him my garage and the old classics I'm working on there."

"Wow!" exclaimed Mr. Silverhorse. "That's a hard offer to resist. I love old cars, too."

Before Miss Kotter left, she gave each of the PTs 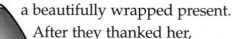 a beautifully wrapped present. After they thanked her, LaToya's mom said, "No one should be alone on Christmas Eve. Would you like to spend the night at our house?"

Miss Kotter smiled. "Thank you so much for the offer. But I'm going to call Whispering Pines and see if they'll put up a cot for me in Ma Jones' room so we can spend the night together — just like when I was a little girl."

Suzie clapped. "This is better than a movie!"

"All right," Mrs. Thomas replied. "But we'll be expecting you for Christmas dinner tomorrow!"

By the time Petie hung up his stocking and everyone finally got to bed at Sam's house that night, it was almost midnight. Sam lay for a while on the couch watching the twinkling Christmas tree lights. And thinking.

For weeks and weeks she had dreamed of Christmas. And now it was almost here. How things had changed during that time! Her dad had lost his job and got another one. And now that job was over, too. They had found an injured dog — and Sonya and her dad, too. Miss Kotter had lost her boyfriend. Yet she had found new friends, too, and she looked happily content.

And look how God helped Sam and her friends put on that Christmas camp! They never could have done it by themselves.

Thank You, God, Sam prayed. *Thanks for everything. But especially for my best friend, Jesus. Merry Christmas!*

· Good News · from God's Word

Christmas has always been a time for showing love, especially that very first Christmas night.

Mary Welcomes the Shepherds and Wise Men

FROM MATTHEW 2:1-12; LUKE 2:1-20

Do you enjoy having guests at your home for Christmas? How about going somewhere to be a guest yourself?

Well, that very first Christmas night Mary and Joseph had a lot of company. Visitors they hadn't even invited!

Think how you'd feel. Mary and Joseph were

far away from home. The only place to stay was a
stable! They had no family or friends in town. No
food, nor a place to cook it or serve it. No bed to
sleep in. And on top of that, they had a brand-new
baby to take care of!

But that baby was a very special baby: God's
own Son. The angels proclaimed the glad news to the
shepherds. So the shepherds came running to see Him.

Some wise men lived far away. They had been
looking for God to send Jesus. When they saw the
special, bright star in the sky, they hurried to come,
too, and brought gifts for the baby. We don't know
how long it took them to get there, maybe a day or
two, maybe a year. But they showed up to be Mary
and Joseph's guests, too.

And you know something? Even though Mary
and Joseph had no fine furniture or grand food to

share, they welcomed all these strangers as friends because these people all loved God. Mary and Joseph did, too. They knew that God would want them to allow others to share this Good News about Jesus, just as we can share that Good News today.

A Verse to Remember

For to us a child is born, to us a son is given.

— Isaiah 9:6

What About You?

What is your favorite thing about Christmas? Do you ever get together with relatives or other guests? Write about your very best Christmas here:

_____

_____

_____

_____

_____

_____

_____

The Very First Christmas Night

   Draw a picture of the very first Christmas night in the box below or on another sheet of paper. You can color it with crayons, paints, colored pencils or markers. You may also add glue and sprinkle glitter (but if you do, be sure to allow your picture time to dry). Then share your picture with your family or a friend.

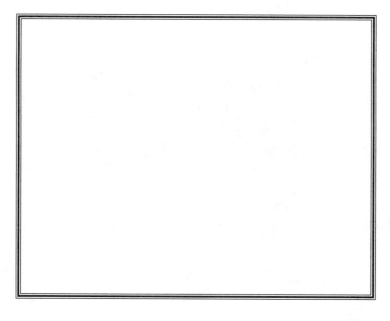

Advent Calendar

   Cut out or copy the wise men and paste them onto Day 17 on your Advent calendar. This picture shows the wise men with their gifts for baby Jesus. The Secret Letter for chapter 17 is "E" for "excited about God's work." Write it on line 2.

Chapter 18

Merry Christmas!

Sam thought she was too excited to sleep a wink on Christmas Eve. But the next thing she knew, Petie was shaking her awake. It was still pitch black outside, but he kept whispering, "Wake up, Sam! It's Christmas already. Look at what's under the tree!"

They turned on the Christmas tree lights. "Wow!" Sam whispered back. *Where did all those gifts come from,* she thought. She was right there in the living room all night and never heard a thing!

"I thought Christmas would be impossible this year," Sam said. "Boy, I wish we could start opening everything right now!"

Mrs. Pearson walked in, still wearing her robe.

"Breakfast first, kids," she reminded them.

"But I'm not hungry!" Petie whined. But Mrs. Pearson soon had ready plates full of scrambled eggs and French toast with syrup. When he saw the delicious food, Petie suddenly changed his mind about breakfast. In fact, he asked if he could lead the blessing himself!

Mr. Pearson got out his camera and Grandma and Grandpa came in to the living room, too. Then Petie got to open his first present. He loved every one of them, including a mysterious note that read:

For something that will really zoom,
look down in the basement rec room.

"A new bike!" he squealed as he spied the bike downstairs. "A new red bike! Now I don't have to ride Sam's old one!" He jumped on the shiny bike and rode it all over the basement.

Sam loved her presents, too. A delicate string of artificial pearls from her parents. A new sweater for school — the one she wanted! Even Petie had a special gift for her, a note that read:

I will help with the dishes and not gripp about it.
Merry Christmas,
Petie

He had misspelled "gripe," of course, but Sam hugged him anyway.

But her most special present was a gorgeous party dress Grandma Pearson had made for her. The velvet and taffeta fabric in the dress were the same blue as Sam's eyes. The dress had a high collar, puffy shoulders and a large bow in the back.

"It's so pretty, Grandma!" she cried. She hugged her grandmother, then ran right upstairs to put it on. It fit perfectly!

Only one of her presents was left unopened — the one from Miss Kotter. She wanted to wait until her teacher was there to open that.

Sam's parents and grandparents loved their presents, too. Even Sneezit got a new chew toy and a new sweater to wear outside. He promptly started chewing on the sweater instead, though. "I think he wants to wear it on the inside," Sam laughed, as she took it away from him.

By now the sun was up. It was a beautiful winter day. Just then the phone rang. It was Maria's mother. "I've made lots of extra tamales," she said. "Everyone's welcome to come over any time. Lolita and the twins are dying to show off their new toys."

"What a great idea!" Sam's mother replied. "We have oodles to eat here, too. And Christine Thomas said they did, too. Why don't we have a Christmas pot luck party?"

More phone calls followed. Soon all the PTs' families had invited each other to stop by. Even Le's mom's new boyfriend and Mrs. Greenleaf and her new roommate, Mrs. Ryan, were invited.

By noon people were flowing in and out of
Sam's house. So much so, it was hard to keep the
front doors closed and the snow out. Suzie's
family came, bringing lots of presents,
including a new collar for Sneezit and a new
snowboard for Sam and Petie.

Sonya dropped by with Cocky. Cocky and
Sneezit had fun playing together. Sam's dad
eventually put the two dogs down in the basement to
play so people wouldn't keep tripping over them. It
was a noisy, bubbly crowd!

Now only Miss Kotter, Sonya's dad and Le's
family hadn't stopped in yet. "Le said she and her
mom would be by later," Sam said. "Miss Kotter is still
at Whispering Pines with Ma Jones. Mr. Silverhorse
said he'll bring her over after he takes care of some
business."

Then Sam and her PTs went around to each
other's homes to check out the food and gifts. They
all raved over Sam's new dress. Le did, too, when she
arrived with her mom and Mrs. Tran's new friend
and his sons.

The little boys, Nicholas and Michael, were
soon running around in the Pearsons' rec room with
the dogs, Petie and Maria's little brothers. Jenna's little
sister Katie played upstairs with Suzie and Lolita. Mrs.
Jenkins, of course, was home with her new babies. But
everyone called to wish her a merry Christmas.

Meanwhile, Grandma Pearson, Mrs. Ryan and
Mrs. Greenleaf all sat at LaToya's house with Granny B.

sipping tea and swapping stories and recipes.

Finally, Miss Kotter and Mr. Silverhorse arrived. Miss Kotter thanked the girls for her special calendar and told how much Ma Jones enjoyed looking at it. Then the PTs opened her presents to them: gold chains with tiny hearts that spelled P-T-4-J.

"What is...?" Sara started.

But Sonya knew the answer right away. "Ponytails for Jesus!" she exclaimed. "Right?"

"Right!" Miss Kotter laughed. She helped all the girls put on their new necklaces.

Meanwhile, Mr. Silverhorse had been talking with Sam's and Maria's fathers out in Mr. Moreno's garage. When they returned to Sam's house, all three were smiling.

"I have an announcement, folks," Sonya's father began. "You know I work for SuperService Automotive. We're looking for qualified people to manage auto repair shops for us. Well, I found our two new managers for Circleville and got the financing arranged for them. And here are those two new managers: Pedro Moreno and Joe Pearson!" Sam's dad had a new job!

Sam burst into tears of joy. "Oh, Miss Kotter!" she blubbered. "I thought Christmas was impossible this year. And look what happened!"

Her teacher hugged her. "Yes, I thought it would be impossible for me, too, after that letter from

Bob. Instead, this is my very best Christmas ever. For 'with God all things are possible.' "

Even impossible Christmas presents!

· Good News · from God's Word

Sam wasn't the only one who had a joyful day after God helped her family through their problems. So did Mary, long ago, in our special Bible story.

Mary's Happy Day

FROM MATTHEW 2:13-23

Before the wise men found Mary and Joseph and baby Jesus in Bethlehem, they told King Herod that they were looking for the new king. "Please come back and tell me where the new king is when you find him!" Herod cried. "I want to go and worship Him, too!"

But Herod was lying. He was a very evil man who killed many people. He wanted to kill this new king, too.

So God told the wise men to go home by another way and to not tell Herod where baby Jesus was. That made Herod so angry he ordered all the baby boys in Bethlehem to be killed.

But he still didn't find baby Jesus. God had already told Joseph in a dream to take Mary and baby Jesus to Egypt, where Jesus would be safe from Herod's law. They stayed in Egypt, safe and sound.

The people in Egypt were good to them, but Mary was homesick. Egypt wasn't her home. Neither was Bethlehem. Nazareth was. She wanted to go back to Nazareth and show off her new baby to all her relatives, including Elizabeth. Her husband, Joseph, wanted to get back to working as a carpenter. They wanted to worship God with their friends and family.

Finally, one day Joseph had another important dream. In the dream, God told him, "Herod is dead now. You can go back home to Nazareth."

They traveled many days, probably riding little donkeys. Finally, Mary could look up the road and see her hometown. "Thank You, God, for taking care of us!" she prayed.

A Verse to Remember

They will call him Immanuel —
which means, "God with us."

—*Matthew 1:23*

What About You?

Do you have a friend or family member who needs to realize how much God loves him or her? Someone who needs to tell God "thank You"? A person who needs to be encouraged by knowing all of what God wants to do for him or her? Maybe you can think of more than one person like that. Write the name or names here and what each person needs to be reminded about God:

_____

_____

_____

_____

Write today's date: _____

Now start praying for that person or those persons. Remember, as Sam found out, with God nothing is impossible!

Sam, Party Girl

Here is the new party dress Sam's grandmother made for her. You can color it and decorate it as you wish (or copy it onto another sheet).

PT4J

Here are PT4J necklaces for you to make. Color and cut out the hearts, or copy them onto card stock. Punch a hole in the top of each one where indicated. Thread a length of gold wrapping twine or satin ribbon through each hole. Keep one for yourself and give the other to a friend!

Advent Calendar

   Cut out or copy the church bells and glue them onto the Day 18 spot on your Advent calendar. This picture shows church bells ringing for joy at Christmas. The Secret Letter for chapter 18 is "S" for "showing gratitude." Write it on line 10.

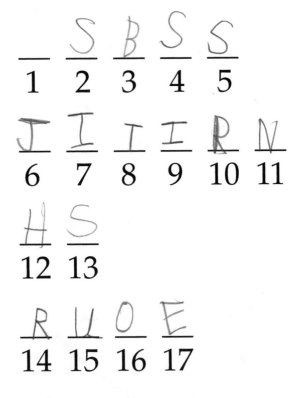

   Note: You now have all the secret letters you need for the secret message on your Advent calendar. Write those secret letters in order from 1-17 on the lines below. What is the Secret Message? See page 203 for the solution!

_	S	B	S	S
1	2	3	4	5

J	I	I	I	R	N
6	7	8	9	10	11

H	S
12	13

R	U	O	E
14	15	16	17

Extra Stuff!

The following pages contain bonus Ponytail Girls activities especially for you. In this section you will find information on forming your own Ponytail Girls Club, including membership cards.

At the end of this section, be sure to check out the coupon for a **free scrunchie!**

My Favorite PT

You have now met and adventured with seven PTs: Sam, Sara, LaToya, Le, Maria, Jenna, and Sonya. You've laughed with them, cried with them, prayed with them and rejoiced with them.

Which PT is your favorite? Maybe she's the PT who is the most like you are. Or perhaps she's the PT who is the most like the way you hope to be.

Here's your chance to write about which PT you like best and why. On the back of this page, draw her picture. Then draw yourself right beside her. Try cutting your face from a small picture (get permission first) and glue it over your drawn one.

_____

_____

_____

_____

_____

_____

My Favorite PT and Me

The Ponytail Girls Club

Would you like to be a part of a Ponytail Girls Club? You can be a PT yourself, of course. But it's much more fun if one of your friends joins with you. Or even five or six of them! There is no cost. You can read the Ponytail Girls stories together, do the puzzles and other activities, study the Bible stories, and learn the Bible verses.

If your friends buy their own Ponytail Girls books, you can all write in yours at the same time. Arrange a regular meeting time and place, and plan to do special things together, just like the PTs do in the stories, such as shopping, Bible study, homework, or helping others.

Trace or copy the membership cards on page 195 and give one to each PT in your group.

Membership Cards

Trace or photocopy these cards. Fill them out, date them, and give one to each member of your Ponytail Girls Club. Be sure to put your membership card in your wallet or another special place for safekeeping!

_____

is a member in good standing of
The Ponytail Girls Club.

_____
Signature

_____
Date

_____

is a member in good standing of
The Ponytail Girls Club.

_____
Signature

_____
Date

Bible Verses to Remember and Share

These are the Bible verses the PTs studied throughout this book. Write them on pretty paper and learn them. Share your favorite with someone else!

Praise the Lord, for the Lord is good.
~ Psalm 35:3

Praise awaits you, O God,…O you who hear prayer.
~ Psalm 65:1-2

Whatever your hand finds to do,
do it with all your might.
~ Ecclesiastes 9:10

For unto us a child is born, to us a son is given.
~ Isaiah 9:6

You are to give him the name Jesus, because he will
save his people from their sins.
~ Matthew 1:21

They will call him Immanuel —
which means, "God with us."
~ Matthew 1:23

Nothing is impossible with God.
~ Luke 1:37

A Savior has been born to you; he is Christ the Lord.
~ Luke 2:11

continued on next page…

For God so loved the world that
he gave his one and only Son.
~ John 3:16

We know that in all things God works
for the good of those who love him.
~ Romans 8:28

Carry each other's burdens.
~ Galatians 6:2

Be kind and compassionate to one another,
forgiving each other.
~ Ephesians 4:32

Be strong in the Lord and in his mighty power.
~ Ephesians 6:10

For to me, to live is Christ.
~ Philippians 1:21

Join with others in following my example.
~ Philippians 3:17

We have put our hope in the living God.
~ 1 Timothy 4:10

Keep…sound teaching,
with faith and love in Christ Jesus.
~ 2 Timothy 1:13

Whoever claims to live in him
must walk as Jesus did.
~ 1 John 2:6

Glossary (glos/ə rē)

Ahaziah: *a-huh-zie-uh*

Appliqued: *ap-pluh-kayed*

Athaliah: *ath-uh-lie-uh*

Capernaum: *kuh-purr-num*

Cheerio: *cheer-ee-o*

Gracias: thank you

Hagar: *hay-gar*

Ishmael: *ish-may-el*

Jehoida: *juh-hoy-duh*

Jehosheba: *jeh-HO-shuh-buh*

Jericho: *jer-uh-ko*

Joash: *joe-ash*

Koala: *kuh-wall-uh*

Niño: little boy

Perro: dog

Posada: *po-sah-duh*

Rahab: *ray-hab*

Sí: yes

Ta-da: *tuh-daw*

Ukulele: *u-kuh-lay-lee*

Zechariah: *zeck-uh-ri-uh*

Zipporah: *zip-pour-uh*

Answers to Puzzles

Chapter 2
You're a Superhero!, p. 33
Always ask God to help you.

Chapter 3
Here We Go A-Caroling!, p. 41
1. d
2. g
3. e
4. f
5. h
6. j
7. b
8. a
9. c
10. i

Chapter 4
O Christmas Tree!, p. 53
J
ES
US
GODS
CHRI
STMAS
GIFT
OF LOVE

Chapter 6
Rhoda's Praise Maze, pp. 70-71

Chapter 10
God's Blessings Word Search, p. 109

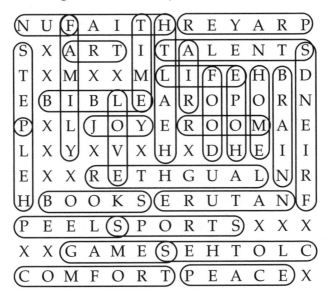

Chapter 11
What About You?, p. 118
1. c
2. c
3. b

Chapter 13
Where Will It All End?, p. 140
Betty, Yvonne, Edward, Daniel, Linda, Adrian, Ned, Donna, Anne, Esther, Rosa, Art, Tom, Mitch, Heather, Rick, Kurt, Tyler, Rob, Briana, Angela, Andy

Chapter 15
Everything But the Kitchen Sink, pp. 159-160
1. D
2. I
3. F
4. A
5. G
6. C
7. J
8. B
9. H
10. E

Chapter 18
Advent Calendar, p. 188
JESUS CHRIST IS BORN

GET A FREE SCRUNCHIE!

The Ponytail Girls love to give each other gifts. Here is one for you: a free scrunchie! Just fill out the form below and enclose a check or money order for $2.20 to cover shipping and handling. Also, we would love to hear more about you and your thoughts, so please fill out the form on the other side, too.

☐ Send my friend a free catalog, too!

My name _____

My address _____

City _____ State _____ Zip _____

My friend's name _____

Address _____

City _____ State _____ Zip _____

Parent's signature _____

My birth date: ____ / ____ / ____
            month/day/year

☐ Send me a scrunchie and a free catalog!
My check or money order for $2.20 is enclosed.

Mail this form to: Ponytails • Legacy Press • P.O. Box 261129 • San Diego, CA 92196

Which of The Ponytail Girls books have you read?

- [ ] *Meet the Ponytail Girls*
- [x] *The Impossible Christmas Present*
- [ ] *Lost on Monster Mountain*
- [ ] *A Stormy Spring*
- [ ] *Escape from Camp Porcupine*

My favorite PT is: Sam

I am in a Ponytail Girls Club. [ ] yes [x] no

I am in another club. [ ] yes [x] no

The name of my club is: Girls Rule

My favorite thing to do is: Out of the Blue

My favorite book is: Out of the Blue
because: it has horses in it and I love them

My favorite magazine is: Ranger Rick
because: It has lots of documentaries about animals

The fun devotional that helps girls grow closer to God.

God and Me! is a series of devotionals for girls. Each age-level book is packed with over 100 devotionals, plus memory verses, stories, journal space and fun activities to help you learn more about the Bible.

LP46823
ISBN 1-885358-54-7

LP46822
ISBN 1-885358-60-1

National Best-sellers!

LP46821
ISBN 1-885358-61-X

Attention: Christian babysitters!

This is the only manual you will need to be the best babysitter on the block— and to share about God with others. *The Official Christian Babysitting Guide* is packed with everything you want to know about taking care of kids. Step-by-step instructions will help you learn the best ways to change a diaper, feed a baby or calm a scared child. Plus, get ideas for keeping kids busy with pages and pages of crafts, games, snacks and songs. Most importantly, you will find Scriptures and strategies for serving God as you serve families. Get *The Official Christian Babysitting Guide* and find out how you can be a blessing as you babysit!

LP 48021
ISBN 1-58411-027-9

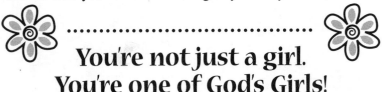

You're not just a girl.
You're one of God's Girls!

Hey, girls, get ready to add some sparkle to your look and a lot of fun to your life. *God's Girls* is packed with tips and ideas to help you make cool crafts. Plus you will read about Bible women and learn how to be a faithful Christian. There is even space included for you to write your deepest thoughts and dreams. So come on and join the party...you are one of *God's Girls!*

LP48011
ISBN 1-58411-020-1

LP48012
ISBN 1-58411-021-X